At Issue

How Should the World Respond to Natural Disasters?

Other books in the At Issue series:

Antidepressants
Are American Elections Fair?
Are Privacy Rights Being Violated?
Biological and Chemical Weapons
Child Labor and Sweatshops
Child Sexual Abuse
Creationism Versus Evolution
Does Advertising Promote Substance Abuse?
Does the World Hate the United States?
Do Infectious Diseases Pose a Serious Threat?
Do Nuclear Weapons Pose a Serious Threat?
Drug Testing
The Ethics of Capital Punishment
The Ethics of Euthanasia
The Ethics of Genetic Engineering
The Ethics of Human Cloning
Gay and Lesbian Families
Gay Marriage
Gene Therapy
How Can Domestic Violence Be Prevented?
How Does Religion Influence Politics?
Hurricane Katrina
Is the Mafia Still a Force in America?
Is Poverty a Serious Threat?
Legalizing Drugs
Prescription Drugs
Responding to the AIDS Epidemic
School Shootings
Steroids
What Causes Addiction?

At Issue

How Should the World Respond to Natural Disasters?

Rebecca K. O'Connor, Book Editor

GREENHAVEN PRESS

An imprint of Thomson Gale, a part of The Thomson Corporation

THOMSON

™

GALE

Detroit • New York • San Francisco • San Diego • New Haven, Conn.
Waterville, Maine • London • Munich

©2006 Thomson Gale, a part of The Thomson Corporation.

Thomson and Star Logo are trademarks and Gale and Greenhaven Press are registered trademarks used herein under license.

For more information, contact:
Greenhaven Press
27500 Drake Rd.
Farmington Hills, MI 48331-3535
Or you can visit our Internet site at http://www.gale.com

Cover photographs reproduced by permission of © PhotoDisc/StockPhotos.com/Corel.

LIBRARY OF CONGRESS CATALOGING-IN-PUBLICATION DATA

How should the world respond to natural disasters? / Rebecca K. O'Connor, book editor.
    p. cm. -- (At Issue)
    Includes bibliographical references and index.
    ISBN 0-7377-3383-7 (lib. bdg. : alk. paper) -- ISBN 0-7377-3384-5 (pbk. : alk. paper) 1. Natural disaster warning systems. 2. Disaster relief. 3. Emergency management I. O'Connor, Rebecca. II. At issue (San Diego, Calif.)
    GB5030.H69 2006
    363.34'525--dc22
                                                        2005045633

Printed in the United States of America
10 9 8 7 6 5 4 3 2 1

Contents

Introduction   **7**

1. The International Response to Natural   **11**
   Disasters Must Be Improved
   Ed Tsui

2. International Donors Save Many Lives   **19**
   UNICEF

3. International Efforts to Limit the   **23**
   Devastation of Natural Disasters Are
   Inadequate
   Emma Young

4. An Indian Ocean Tsunami Warning   **29**
   System Must Be Developed
   Costas Synolakis

5. Creating an Indian Ocean Tsunami   **36**
   Warning System Is Futile
   Keith Alverson

6. Developing Countries Lack Adequate   **43**
   Disaster Prevention and Recovery
   Programs
   Suprakash Roy

7. Developed Nations Must Help Poorer   **48**
   Countries Modernize
   Ross Clark

8. Trauma Counseling Helps Disaster   **53**
   Victims
   Sherwin B. Nuland

9. Trauma Counseling May Not Help   **62**
   Victims
   Erzulie Coquillon

10. The U.S. Government's Response to
    Disasters Discriminates Against the Poor
    and Minorities
    Ted Steinberg   66

11. Nations Should Provide Aid for
    Humanitarian Reasons Alone
    The Economist   76

12. Developers Should Build More Carefully
    on Coastlines
    *David M. Bush, William J. Neal, and
    Robert S. Young*   82

13. People Should Not Live in Hazard-Prone
    Areas
    Seth R. Reice   89

14. Relief Agencies Must Dispel Myths About
    Natural Disasters
    Claude de Ville de Goyet   94

15. Relief Agencies Should Study Past
    Disasters
    Thomas R. DeGregori   99

16. Hurricane Katrina Revealed the
    Weakness of U.S. Emergency Response
    Paul Light   109

17. A Belief in God Can Protect Against
    Disasters
    John Ross Schroeder   114

Organizations to Contact   122

Bibliography   127

Index   135

Introduction

On December 26, 2004, a "megathrust quake," which results from the sinking of one tectonic plate below the other, occurred eleven miles below the surface of the Indian Ocean. This sudden shifting of land beneath the ocean displaced a tremendous amount of water, sending it hurtling toward southern Asia and eastern Africa at 620 miles per hour. In some places these waves were as high as fifty feet, causing massive devastation, especially in Indonesia, Thailand, Sri Lanka, and India. There are 182,340 confirmed deaths and 129,897 people missing, making this tsunami one of the worst natural disasters on record. In Indonesia alone, 280,000 buildings were destroyed or damaged, 800,000 people were left homeless and 500,000 lost their livelihoods.

The world's response to the disaster was unprecedented in its immediacy and generosity. Governments pledged $7 billion to aid the victims of the tsunami, and another $5 billion was donated by private individuals, companies, foundations, and religious groups. However, after a tragedy of such magnitude many people began to reconsider how governments and nongovernmental organizations should respond to natural disasters, including hurricanes, volcanic eruptions, and earthquakes. Although immediate relief following a disaster is critical, experts now agree that the best way for the world to respond is to focus on mitigation efforts to reduce the potential devastation of a natural disaster before it strikes.

One of the lessons of the December 2004 tsunami is the importance of having an early warning system. Had such a system been in place in Southeast Asia, officials would have had between 90 and 150 minutes in which to broadcast warnings by radio, television, and loudspeakers, giving people a chance to escape to higher land. Tens of thousands of lives could have been saved. Experts agree that in the event of a tsunami early warning and evacuation plans are critical. Richard K. Eisner, regional administrator for the California Governor's Office of Emergency Services, points out that tsunami evacuation and response planning is important even in the United States. He notes, "It is estimated that more than 900,000 people in 48 communities in the states of California, Oregon, Washington, Alaska and Hawaii live in areas vulnerable to 50-foot tsunami." Warning systems can also be used to announce hurricanes, cyclones, volcanic eruptions, and other natural disasters.

Proper development and construction in areas prone to disaster is another way that destruction and loss of lives can be mitigated. Buildings that are constructed according to safety codes that require features such as reinforced walls and high quality cement, brick, and wood are more likely to withstand a storm or an earthquake. The collapse of unsafe structures during natural disasters has killed tens of thousands of people over the years, especially those who live in poor areas. As geography professor Marin R. Degg observes, in Peru, a country with frequent destructive earthquakes, "The poorest urban dwellers are often forced to construct their own housing using whatever materials are to hand, leading to poor quality and unplanned housing developments that are vulnerable to disasters."

The design and implementation of building codes can ensure that communities are better able to withstand disaster. However, because high quality construction is more expensive, it is a difficult challenge to implement and enforce building codes, particularly in undeveloped countries. Experts therefore argue that rather than focus on disaster relief, donors should assist in the development of third world countries.

Protecting the natural features of the land can also often help protect communities from natural disasters. In Vietnam, where an average of ten typhoons strikes the coast annually, tidal flooding often breaches the dikes constructed to protect the land. However, by replanting and protecting the natural mangroves the Red Cross has protected miles of coastline. The care and protection of these mangroves has cost $1.1 million; however it has saved $7.3 million in the cost of dike maintenance. David Peppiatt, manager of the ProVention Consortium, an international coalition dedicated to reducing the impact of natural disasters in developing countries states, "Many projects such as the mangrove planting in Vietnam illustrate that investment in disaster reduction measures not only reduces the impact of disasters, but also saves money in the response stage."

Unfortunately, there are obstacles to these mitigation efforts. One of the biggest hurdles is people's tendency to put off planning for natural disasters. As Peppiatt states, "Despite the obvious economic arguments, the international community is still more inclined to repair than prepare." Even in the United States there is a history of responding rather than preparing. For example, engineers knew that the levee system in New Orleans, Louisiana, could not withstand a hurricane above a Category 3, yet did not fix the problem. They experienced their worst fears as the city flooded following Katrina, a Category 4 hurricane, in September 2005.

Another challenge to developing early warning systems and other mitigation techniques is getting multiple countries to agree about and coordinate international projects. Countries are also likely to consider only their own best interest in the development of natural disaster detection and warning systems.

Following Hurricane Katrina, the worst natural disaster in the United States since at least 1900, disaster response experts will certainly be taking an even harder look at disaster preplanning and mitigation. Although New Orleans had an early warning system and an evacuation plan, the government response was disorganized and ineffective, and many residents chose to ignore the evacuation mandate. Worse, the least mobile residents lived in the most flood-prone part of town. Many people simply were unable to leave, and thousands of lives were lost. The preplanning that had been done was inadequate, proving that even developed countries such as the United States need to focus further on disaster mitigation. As David Peppiatt concludes, "Staying a step ahead of disaster is becoming ever more important. Emergency response is vital, but reducing risk in the first place is key."

1

The International Response to Natural Disasters Must Be Improved

Ed Tsui

Ed Tsui is the director of the Office of the Coordinator of Humanitarian Affairs at the United Nations. He joined the United Nations in 1972 and has had extensive experience in the fields of social and economic development and humanitarian affairs. Since 1992 he has been closely involved in organizing and improving international response to humanitarian emergencies and disasters worldwide.

The emergency response to the eruption of Mount Nyirangongo in Africa on January 17, 2002, was highly successful. The reaction to this disaster demonstrated advances in humanitarian efforts and now serves as an example of a well-executed response. The Office for the Coordination of Humanitarian Affairs and many other organizations were involved in the successful relief efforts to the Mount Nyirangongo eruption and have developed a strong understanding of the crucial elements of a successful disaster response. These elements include the immediacy of the response, availability of funds, proper staff and tools, and a coordinated effort between agencies. In the years to come the international humanitarian community must not only continue to im-

Ed Tsui, "Initial Response to Complex Emergencies and Natural Disasters," *Emergency Relief Operations,* edited by Kevin M. Cahill, M.D. New York: Fordham University Press and The Center for International Health and Cooperation, 2003. Copyright © 2003 by The Center for International Health and Cooperation. Reproduced by permission.

prove its response to natural disasters but also work to detect such catastrophes as they occur.

On January 17, 2002, one of Africa's most active volcanoes unexpectedly erupted in the Democratic Republic of Congo (DRC). As lava rapidly advanced toward the lakeside city below, fuel depots erupted into slow burning fires, tremors and shocks crumbled buildings and collapsed houses, heat and lava flows destroyed water and electrical systems, ash covered the landscape, and lava-turned-to-rock covered parts of the lake.

As a result, about 400,000 of Goma town's 500,000 habitants were forced to flee to unstable areas of the DRC and Rwanda, where rebel elements remained active. Nine died and one hundred were wounded. About 40 percent of the town's infrastructure was destroyed, leaving thousands without electricity or potable water.

If ever there were a typical natural disaster, the eruption of Mount Nyirangongo was not it. Its location on a contentious border in an area plagued by armed conflict placed it squarely in the middle of a long-standing, regional, complex emergency, where state and nonstate actors compete for control, misinformation is rampant, and humanitarian access limited.

A number of other factors added to the complexity of the response, including the many actors involved; the threat of further eruptions or factures from associated volcanic *and* seismic activity, whose interplay was classified by both vulcanologists and seismologists alike as a new phenomena; and the potential for contamination of Lake Kivu, a primary source of both food and drinking water in an already impoverished area and, ironically, of noxious gases that threatened to ignite.

Yet the international humanitarian response was as quick as it was comprehensive, and, in spite of the complexity of the situation, largely succeeded in alleviating the immediate needs of those most affected.

Lessons Learned

The Office for the Coordination of Humanitarian Affairs (OCHA) was but one of many players who made this response a success. OCHA and its partners over the past ten years have learned a great deal about the types of tools, mechanisms, and processes needed for an effective emergency response. New technologies, increases in the scope and magnitude of both complex emergencies and natural hazards, as well as the need for common tools to address them, and a growing appreciation by member states of the importance of humanitarian assistance and the protection of civilians to the achievement of peace, security, and development are only a few of the trends that have shaped the nature of emergency response as we know it today. But despite the growing need for humanitarian interventions in ever more complex operating environments, the key lessons learned by the international humanitarian community regarding emergency response in the past decade are straightforward. In short, over time we have come to understand that an effective response depends on the following:

1. Solid needs assessments that allow relief agencies to jointly determine who does what where, under the umbrella of a comprehensive humanitarian action plan

2. The proper staff and emergency response tools available at the right time in the right place

3. Common tools for natural disasters and complex emergencies, which build on the comparative advantage of the other without losing their ability to be applied in unique situations

4. Emergency funding mechanisms that ensure money is readily available and easily dispersed

5. Well-developed information management networks through which accurate-as-possible data are immediately available to key decision-makers

6. Reviews that draw the lessons learned from each response and help apply them to the next

A Successful Example

Each of these lessons was manifested in the Goma response, which included, among other actions, early reinforcements of experienced humanitarian staff, including a senior emergency manager; the provision, through daily updates, of credible and timely information about the crisis at both the field and international levels; the on-site establishment of extraordinary information exchanges and a specialized center to process, analyze, and share humanitarian data; the issuance of an interagency emergency appeal for funds; the rapid dispatch of vulcanologists to the field; and the procurement of emergency nonfood items for the affected population.

As such, this particular response to a sudden onset emergency highlights not only the need for, but also the increasing efforts by, aid actors, in particular OCHA, to ensure that the above elements are consistently at the disposal of the international system, so that each response is timely yet flexible, specialized when needed, and above all, well coordinated.

The international humanitarian response was as quick as it was comprehensive.

As an example of how aid can effectively reach its victims, it also provides a benchmark of comparison to other international emergency responses, where, for whatever reasons, action was neither as swift nor as decisive. Thus, it further highlights the need for greater consistency in the application of the emergency response tools and mechanisms at the disposal of the international humanitarian community.

Before I elaborate on these lessons and themes, it is useful to understand the increasingly challenging and multifaceted backdrop against which aid workers struggle to deliver assistance in the field and that has shaped the formulation of emergency response.

Natural Disaster and Complex Emergencies

In the last two decades alone, more than three million people have died in natural disasters caused by extreme weather resulting from global warming and other related atmospheric changes, as well as by deforestation and soil erosion caused by unsustainable development practices. Combined with poverty and population pressure, growing numbers of people are being forced to live in harm's way—on flood plains, unstable hillsides, and earthquake-prone zones.

Similarly, the end of the Cold War has resulted in profound changes not only in the number but also in the nature of armed, internal conflicts. In the last decade of the twentieth century, regions once thought to be beyond war, such as Western Europe, became entrenched in it; simmering socioeconomic tensions in many African countries resurfaced; and the war on terrorism gave way to far-reaching humanitarian implications in Central Asia and the Middle East. In this period, conflicts have claimed more than five million lives and driven many times that number of people from their homes. At present, it is estimated that more than 40 million people have been displaced by conflict worldwide.

Increasingly, as we saw in Goma, the traditional distinctions between the two types of crises—natural disasters and complex emergencies—are not always so clear. Interplay between the two has become common. This is particularly true in the case of drought, which differs from most natural disasters in that it is slow in onset and may continue for a prolonged period of time, which can lead to a conflict over scarce resources. In ongoing emergencies, drought can also exacerbate existing tensions.

Whatever the cause, the resulting effects of these emergencies are similar. They include extensive violence and loss of life, increasingly among innocent noncombatants and civilians, massive displacements of people, and widespread damage to societies and economies. But despite the similarities, key differences in the immediacy, duration, scope, and political complexity of a crisis have increasingly called for specialized capacities or services in the initial response.

Immediacy In the event of a natural disaster, such as an earthquake or volcano, thousands of lives are put at immediate risk. Many can be lost within hours or days of the incident if search and rescue and other life-saving efforts are delayed. In these cases, a rapid initial response is critical, and often more easily applicable, to the goal of saving lives.

Complex emergencies, on the other hand, are characterized by a total or considerable breakdown of authority. They usually involve more deliberate violence—and therefore violations of human rights and international humanitarian law—targeted at civilians, as well as political and military constraints that hinder response and pose more significant and sinister security risks to aid workers. Aid actors are not always able to reach populations, and the type of assistance required is often varied. For instance, immediate, on-the-spot assistance can consist of medical treatment for war-related injuries. But this is often combined with sustained and cumulative needs, arising from weeks and months of deprivation due to lack of access to basic social services and food, over long periods of time. Thus, the provision of timely assistance may be as critical, but the operating environments are usually more complex and require a more tailored response.

Duration As a result of these differences in immediacy, the life-saving stage that follows a natural disaster response may be over within a matter of days or weeks, notwithstanding the reconstruction efforts that may follow.

The chronic humanitarian needs arising from war, however, often continue for months and even years. Additionally, as the nature of an emergency changes—for example, from the immediate aftermath of military action, to a long-simmering standoff between government and militant groups, to a negotiated peace—humanitarian assistance programs may evolve and become more varied, encompassing simultaneous relief programs as well as rehabilitation and reintegration activities. These situations necessitate longer-term initiatives designed to minimize human suffering over time.

Scope Natural disasters increasingly span several countries. For instance, when successive cyclones hit southeastern Africa in February 2001, rivers and dams overflowed throughout the region, resulting in widespread flooding in Mozambique, Swaziland, Botswana, Malawi, Zimbabwe, and South Africa, affecting more than two million people. But although several neighboring countries can be affected by the same natural disaster, especially in case of drought, their relationships are not always strained, and cooperation is more common.

In the event of a natural disaster, such as an earthquake or volcano, thousands of lives are put at immediate risk.

In complex emergency situations, however, the international and cross-border dimensions are almost always characterized by political differences between those concerned. One need not look further than the former Federal Republic of Yugoslavia, the Great Lakes region of Africa, or the West African subregion for examples of how conflict spreads, displacing thousands in a tangled web of cross-border movements. Responding to such crises requires a higher level of regional coordination and interaction with a greater multiplicity of actors, who are often at odds with each other. . . .

17

Continuing to Make Progress

Through this combination of shared experience, the international humanitarian community has in the last decade made great strides in its efforts to create a common platform of response practices and tools. Overall, it is reacting more quickly and in a more coordinated manner to bring relief to the victims of disasters and emergencies. But as the war on terrorism and other sources of conflict continue, we are certain to face ever increasing and perhaps unanticipated challenges in the delivery of humanitarian assistance. To that end, we must look beyond improvements in how we respond to crisis. We must learn to be quicker to detect and prepare for crises before they occur. The earlier we intervene, the more likely we are able to have a meaningful impact on the ground. Similarly, we must more consistently enter all crisis situations with a clearly defined and viable exit strategy that guides all of our actions, even in the initial response, toward the ultimate stability and recovery of the affected country. Greater advocacy efforts before, during, and after an acute crisis can also help us to better harness public and political attention, especially in the early days of a crisis when international attention is highest. The very fluidity of the situations in which we work has forced us to remain flexible, and that has led to many improvements in our response. In the coming years, we must continue to demonstrate the same level of versatility and ability to learn from our past interventions so that we may ultimately save more lives.

2

International Donors Save Many Lives

UNICEF

The United Nations Children's Fund (UNICEF) was founded in 1946 to save, protect, and improve the lives of children in 157 countries. UNICEF achieves these goals by providing immunization, education, health care, nutrition, clean water, and sanitation.

After the December 2004 tsunami, people feared that epidemics and chaos would erupt in the countries devastated by the tragedy. However, due to the swift response of relief agencies, these problems did not materialize. In fact, in the six months following the tsunami, there were no outbreaks of cholera, measles, or typhoid, the three major diseases likely to occur after a disaster of this magnitude. Although historically, many children die from these diseases in the event of a major disaster, internationally funded relief agencies like UNICEF were able to prevent their occurrence by providing immunization and vitamin supplementation. UNICEF has also helped to provide clean, safe water, basic sanitation, housing for orphans, food for malnourished children and pregnant women, and school supplies. UNICEF would not have been able to respond to the crisis so effectively without the contributions of donors from around the world.

UNICEF, "No Cholera, No Measles, No Typhoid: Six Months After the Tsunami, UNICEF Reports Rapid Donor Response Saved Children's Lives," June 22, 2005.

A s the six-month anniversary of the South Asia tsunami [of 2004] approaches, the U.S. Fund for UNICEF is reporting that the heroic efforts of concerned donors has helped make the recovery efforts a success. Following the worst natural disaster in living memory, there were early fears of a disease epidemic, trafficking of children, and chaos within the aid community—all of which have failed to materialize.

In the relatively short period of time that has elapsed, tangible signs of recovery are present. For example,

- 90 percent of affected children have returned to school. More than 561,000 children are learning again with the help of UNICEF's "School-in-a-Box" kits and UNICEF has paid for the rehabilitation of 1,573 schools.

- An estimated 211,000 children have benefited from psychosocial support organized by UNICEF.

- To prevent malaria, UNICEF provided 240,000 people with bed nets.

- And most importantly, safe water which helps to prevent disease—is reaching more than one million people a day by UNICEF.

Many Children Saved

The most remarkable outcome of the relief efforts is that no children have died as a result of cholera, measles and typhoid attributable to the tsunami crisis. "The most remarkable outcome of the relief efforts is that no children have died as a result of cholera, measles and typhoid attributable to the tsunami crisis," said Charles J. Lyons, President of the U.S. Fund for UNICEF. "When the disaster first struck, we were gravely concerned by the likelihood of an epidemic, but UNICEF averted outbreaks of those preventable diseases thanks to our donors' generosity. Had donors not come through so quickly, many more children would have died."

Historically, children die from diseases that strike after a natural disaster, but UNICEF's pre-tsunami work helped to prevent an outbreak of child-killing diseases post-tsunami. As part of the recovery work, UNICEF has immunized approximately 1,200,000 children against measles. UNICEF has also distributed bed nets to stem the spread of malaria and provided nearly 850,000 children with vitamin A supplementation.

Without the help of donors, UNICEF would not have been able to respond to the crisis with such swiftness.

While the immediate relief phase is over, there is still much that needs to be done within the affected countries to see that communities are rebuilt and the livelihoods of the people are restored. Additionally, greater efforts are needed to protect the most vulnerable, including women and children. Within the next six months, UNICEF and its partners will continue to provide:

- An ongoing supply of clean, safe water and support for basic sanitation
- Immunizations to prevent fatal childhood diseases
- Special feeding for malnourished children and pregnant women
- Training to help adults identify and care for traumatized children
- Shelter and protection for orphans
- Education kits, school supplies and temporary classrooms
- UNICEF is also rehabilitating, refurbishing damaged schools and constructing new schools

UNICEF quickly recognized that throughout its recovery efforts there is an extraordinary opportunity to improve the quality of life that previously existed within the affected areas and to address the chronic issues plaguing children in the region, such as trafficking and widespread malnutrition. With this in mind, UNICEF has quickly implemented a recovery guideline—"Build Back Better." Wherever possible, UNICEF will help rebuild health and education services to a higher standard than was available before the tsunami, creating better opportunities for children and their families.

Donor Response

The devastation from the earthquake and the resulting tsunami has prompted the most ambitious and perhaps generous international response in history. Without the help of donors, UNICEF would not have been able to respond to the crisis with such swiftness, neither would it have accomplished so much to date and continue to plan for long-term projects. Globally, UNICEF generated over $500 million in funding for the affected countries. The U.S. Fund for UNICEF raised a record $130 million in contributions from children, corporations, faith based organizations, foundations and individuals in less than four months. This is the largest and swiftest outpouring of donations in its nearly 60-year history. Children in the United States alone raised over $12 million for UNICEF's relief and recovery efforts. This figure is unprecedented and a testament to the determination and generosity of children to raise funds to help children and families around the world.

3

International Efforts to Limit the Devastation of Natural Disasters Are Inadequate

Emma Young

Emma Young is a staff writer for New Scientist *and lives in Australia.*

Despite the massive destruction and thousands of deaths caused by the most cataclysmic natural disaster of modern times, the 2004 tsunami in the Indian Ocean, the world has still not taken many useful steps to develop disaster reduction plans. At the World Conference on Disaster Reduction in Kobe, Japan, countries could not agree on plans to reduce the loss of lives to natural disaster or even how much money should be spent on such plans. The only point the government committees agreed to was setting up a tsunami early warning system for the Indian Ocean. Effective worldwide response to natural disasters requires a unified effort which has yet to come to fruition. The world needs to learn from past disasters, discovering what works best in preventing and mitigating the devastation of natural disasters.

The people of Kobe know what disaster feels like. The Hanshin-Awaji earthquake that struck the city on 17 January 1995 cost 6,433 lives, destroyed more than half a million homes, and caused 10 trillion yen in damage.

Emma Young, "Quake, Flood, Fire. Will We Be Ready?" *New Scientist,* January 29, 2005, p. 6. Copyright © 2005 by Reed Elsevier Business Publishing, Ltd. Reproduced by permission.

Ten years on, and just three weeks after the Indian Ocean tsunami that killed at least 280,000 people in Asia and Africa, experts and delegates from 168 countries met last week [in January 2005] in the rebuilt Japanese city to discuss how to prevent future natural disasters claiming so many lives. They agreed a series of initiatives designed to give earlier warnings of tsunamis and floods, and a more coordinated response to extreme natural hazards.

A Wasted Opportunity

Despite this, many of those involved say the World Conference on Disaster Reduction was a wasted opportunity. While there was much well-meaning rhetoric, little emerged in the way of firm disaster reduction plans or targets for saving lives. There was not even any agreement on how much money to spend on reducing the death toll caused by earthquakes, floods, droughts and tsunamis.

"The targets at the beginning of this process were very clear and strong and concrete. What we've seen is that over the diplomatic process of reaching a consensus, they have been tremendously watered down. That is an enormous disappointment," says hazard vulnerability expert Ben Wisner of the London School of Economics.

In May 1994, governments meeting in Yokohama, Japan, agreed to a 10-year strategy based on a framework of principles for thinking about the management of natural disasters. There has been clear progress since Yokohama, says Salvano Briceno, head of the UN's International Strategy for Disaster Reduction. Between May 1994 and April 2004 there were some 7100 disasters worldwide resulting from natural hazards, which killed more than 300,000 people and cost $800 billion. Grim as the death toll was, it was about one-third lower than in the decade before. . . .

[The] Kobe meeting was designed to build on this success. The UN hopes the next 10-year plan, running from 2005 until

2015, will reduce that figure by half again, leaving aside the toll from December's Indian Ocean tsunami.

That disaster was naturally high on the conference agenda, and there was initial optimism that the tragedy might galvanise governments into accepting the need for urgent action. "It's mind-boggling that it takes one tsunami affecting 5 million people severely to make the world wake up, when we have 250 million affected [by disasters] every year for the past 10 years," said Jan Egeland, the UN's head of humanitarian affairs, on the second day of the meeting. "Still, we have to use the momentum we have to get going."

The meeting can claim some achievements. It saw the launch of a UN Global Early Warning Programme, which has the ambitious aim of ensuring that early warnings for all natural hazards, from tsunamis to droughts, are put in place worldwide. But there were no firm government commitments apart from an agreement to set up a tsunami early warning system for the Indian Ocean as soon as possible. The basic technology should be up and running within 18 months, UN agencies declared.

The exact form of that technology, and precisely how it could be made part of a global early warning system for other more common hazards, such as cyclones or flash floods, was left for future meetings to thrash out. Whatever form it takes, a warning system is urgently needed, says Michel Jarraud, head of the World Meteorological Association, adding that tsunami warning systems should also be set up in all other regions at risk.

Warning that a disaster is about to happen is only the start. The real challenge, as delegates acknowledged, is getting alerts to every person at risk, and ensuring they know how to respond. "Only 10 per cent of the problem of early warning rests with hardware. Ninety per cent is how you get these messages down to the end user and whether that person can do anything," Wisner says.

Local Involvement

One of the major themes of the conference was exploring how to involve local communities in disaster-management projects. Case studies show that community-based projects can work even in the poorest, most vulnerable parts of the world. For example, more than half of all Indians affected by floods live in the northern state of Bihar. The last major floods, in July 2004, killed 585 people, affected about 21 million others, and destroyed more than half a million houses. They were caused by dams in Nepal being opened to release water trapped following heavy monsoon rains.

Before the floods struck, a Delhi-based NGO [nongovernmental organization] called the Discipleship Centre had been working with people in Bihar to map vulnerable villages and to formulate response plans such as evacuation routes. Negotiations with landowners persuaded them to allow their workers to move to higher ground when floods struck, which they had previously not permitted. Alex Joseph, who coordinated the project, says villages where such plans were in place suffered fewer deaths and less loss of livestock and property than others in the region.

Warning that a disaster is about to happen is only the start.

In Kobe, governments agreed that every country should have its own disaster management organisation to coordinate suitable projects. There was also recognition that poverty and disasters are often interrelated. Worldwide, about 95 per cent of all deaths in disasters occur in developing countries. And as a percentage of GDP [gross domestic product], losses can be 20 times greater in developing countries than in industrial ones. When hurricane Mitch hit Honduras in 1998 it put back the country's development by 20 years, while the Indian Ocean tsunami will set back the Maldives by an estimated 10 years.

Looking to the Future

Lessons from past disasters are seldom passed on. "We're a bit like a bad football team that, every time it goes out to play, has to learn the rules from scratch," says Andrew Maskrey, chief of the disaster reduction unit of the UN Development Programme's Bureau for Crisis Prevention and Recovery in Geneva, Switzerland. "We need to find a way to move beyond ad hoc interventions to more predictable ways of supporting countries that have suffered a disaster."

Research to discover what works best is urgently needed, says Ian Davis of Cranfield University, UK, who has worked on disaster planning for more than 30 years. One of the few studies so far is being done by the operations evaluation department of the World Bank, which is reviewing the 150 or so reconstruction and disaster mitigation projects the bank ran between 1984 and 2004. The results will be known this year [2005].

Lessons from past disasters are seldom passed on.

At the conference, plans were announced for a partnership to extend this effort. To be financed by Japan, and bringing together several UN agencies and other organisations, the International Recovery Platform (IRP) will, among other things, collect studies into which responses to disaster have worked best. It will also put together teams of experienced experts trained in recovery methods to be dispatched following a disaster. The IRP is "an admirable idea," Davis says. "Let's hope it's a balanced platform—technically, socially and environmentally."

Other initiatives announced at Kobe include an earthquake risk reduction alliance, and an international flood initiative, which aims to carry out more flood research, training and assistance to reduce the loss of life. All, apart from the Indian Ocean early warning system, were agreed in non-government sessions.

But will action really be taken next time it is needed? While the UK and Sweden pushed for hard targets in the Hyogo document, others, including the US, blocked such proposals.

Tellingly, Egeland's opening call for 10 per cent of the $4 to $5 billion spent each year on disaster relief to be earmarked for disaster prevention also failed to find international endorsement. At present only 2 per cent is invested in this way.

4

An Indian Ocean Tsunami Warning System Must Be Developed

Costas Synolakis

Costas Synolakis is a professor of civil, environmental, aerospace, and mechanical engineering at the University of Southern California (USC). He is a member of the USC Tsunami Research Team and has published numerous articles and books on the subject of tsunamis.

Tsunami early warning systems have been developed in response to many tsunami disasters. A 1946 tsunami that destroyed property in Alaska and killed 173 people in Hawaii spurred the creation of the Pacific Tsunami Warning Center. A 1960 Chilean tsunami responsible for the death of more than a thousand people prompted the creation of the International Tsunami Information Center. As more destructive tsunamis occurred, the warning system was further developed. Recent innovations have included the ability to take deep ocean measurements and make more accurate predictions. However, the December 2004 tsunami that developed in the Indian Ocean affected countries that did not have a tsunami warning system because tsunamis have occurred so infrequently in the Indian Ocean (the last one was in 1882). This lack of a warning system led to the deaths of tens of thousands of people. It is now clear that massive tsunamis can develop in the Indian Ocean and that a warning center needs to be created in the region as soon as possible.

In the aftermath of the horrific Asian tsunamis of Dec. 26, [2004] which have killed more than all 20th-century tsunamis combined, many attempts will be made to place blame or quickly "fix" this problem. A little reflection on the history of past reaction to destructive tsunamis may help.

History of Tsunami Warning Systems

The history of tsunami hazard mitigation tracks well with the history of destructive tsunamis in the U.S. Following the 1946 Alaska tsunami that destroyed the Scotch Cap lighthouse in Unimak, Alaska, and then killed 173 people in Hawaii, the Pacific Tsunami Warning Center was established in Hawaii by a predecessor agency to the National Oceanic and Atmospheric Administration.

Following the 1960 Chilean tsunami that killed 1,000 people in Chile, 61 in Hawaii and 199 in Japan, the International Tsunami Information Center, sponsored by the U.N., was formed to coordinate tsunami warning efforts of the Pacific countries. Many research and mitigation efforts were focused on the distant tsunami problem, ignoring the local tsunamis that we now know as far more common. Following the 1964 Alaskan tsunami that killed 120 people in the U.S., the Alaska Tsunami Warning Center in Palmer, Alaska, was established to confront the local tsunami problem. In 1968, the International Coordination Group for the Tsunami Warning System in the Pacific was formed by Unesco. Its purpose was to assure that tsunami watches, warning and advisory bulletins are disseminated throughout the Pacific to member states in accordance with specific procedures. It presently has 26 member states out of the 129 that participate in the U.N. Intergovernmental Oceanographic Commission. No membership fees are required, but a member country has to petition for the service and identify local disaster management officers capable to interpret and act in the event of a tsunami warning.

In 1992, a 7.2 earthquake in California generated a tsunami that killed no one. It was the first subduction zone earthquake recorded on the U.S. West Coast with modern instruments. It triggered concern that larger earthquakes could generate large local tsunamis along the heavily populated West Coast. In response, the National Tsunami Hazard Mitigation Program was formed in 1997.

Warning System Innovations

Two innovations of the program were to create a tsunami forecasting capability and to introduce the concept of tsunami-resilient communities. At the same time, tsunamis started being reported around the Pacific Rim, on average about once a year. The National Science Foundation funded even junior scientists and encouraged them to conduct field surveys to gather data to help validate the models and thus help build the National Oceanic and Atmospheric Administration's forecasting capability. Combined, these innovations constitute a major advance in tsunami hazard mitigation for both local and distant tsunamis. Currently, inundation maps exist for many communities in the U.S.

To forecast tsunamis, tsunami measurements from the deep ocean are required. It took about 30 years to transform the idea of measuring tsunamis in the deep ocean to actually reporting such data in real time. The technical feat of transmitting data from an instrument on the sea floor at great ocean depths to a tsunami warning center in real time required exceptionally creative engineering. The new tsunami measuring technology has given science a new instrument—the tsunameter—that provides tsunami researchers and practitioners with the basic information to understand and predict tsunamis.

The second technology required to predict tsunamis is numerical models of tsunami dynamics. The tsunameter/model combination has transformed the warning function from tsunami detection to tsunami forecasting. In operational use, the tsunameter/model will eventually lead to accurate tsunami forecasts that save lives. Accurate forecasts lead to fewer false alarms that cost in lost productivity and in lost confidence in the warning system.

Unaware of the Danger

The images from Sri Lanka, India and Thailand that have filled our screens—and the descriptions from survivors—are sadly all too familiar, at least to those of us who have conducted tsunami field surveys. At times, some of us thought that we were revisiting images from Flores in 1992, or East Java in 1994, Irian Jaya in 1996, Papua New Guinea in 1998 and Vanuatu in 1999—to just mention catastrophes in countries with similar landscape and coastal construction.

The response of local residents and tourists, however, was unfamiliar, at least to tsunami field scientists for post-1990s tsunamis. In one report, swimmers felt the current associated with the leading depression wave approaching the beach, yet hesitated about getting out of the water because of the "noise" and the fear that there was an earthquake and they would be safer away from buildings. They had to be told by tourists from Japan—a land where an understanding of tsunamis is now almost hard-wired in the genes—to run to high ground. In another report, vacationers spending the day on Phi Phi were taken back to Phuket one hour after the event started. In many cases tsunami waves persist for several hours, and the transport was nothing less than grossly irresponsible.

Contrast these reactions with what happened in Vanuatu, in 1999. On Pentecost Island, a rather pristine enclave with no electricity or running water, the locals watch television once a week, when a pickup truck with a satellite dish, a VCR and a

TV stops by each village. When the International Tsunami Survey Team visited days after the tsunami, they heard that the residents had watched a Unesco video prepared the year before, in the aftermath of the 1998 Papua New Guinea tsunami disaster. When they felt the ground shake during the 1999 earthquake, they ran to a hill nearby. The tsunami swept through, razing the village to the ground. Out of 500 people, only three died, and all three had been unable to run like the others. The tsunami had hit at night.

No Warning

The angry questions that hundreds of thousands of family members of victims are asking, especially in Sri Lanka and India, are "what happened?"—and "why did no one warn us before the tsunami hit?" The Pacific Tsunami Warning Center had issued a tsunami bulletin and had concluded that there was no danger for the Pacific nations in its jurisdiction. Why didn't it extend its warning to South and Southeast Asia? It is perhaps clear with hindsight that an Indian Ocean tsunami warning center should have been in place, or that the Indian Ocean nations should have requested coverage from the Pacific Tsunami Warning Center.

It is perhaps clear with hindsight that an Indian Ocean tsunami warning center should have been in place.

Clearly, the hazard had been grossly underestimated. To give governments the benefit of the doubt, the last transoceanic tsunami that had hit the region was in 1882, and this was caused by Krakatoa's [volcanic] eruption. Other large earthquakes along the Sumatra trench had not caused major tsunamis, or if they had, they had not been reported as devastating. Floods occur nearly every year, as do storms. Natural hazards that are less frequent tend to be ignored. No nation can be ready for every eventuality—as 9/11 painfully demonstrated—at least before a major disaster that identifies the risk. Without the governments of Indian Ocean nations having identified the risk, they probably did not feel they needed the services of the Pacific Tsunami Warning Center, however free. Even simple and inexpensive mitigation strategies such as public education possibly did not even occur as a possibility. The rapid tourist development of Sri Lanka may also have contributed to the government's inaction toward suggesting that some of the region's most beautiful shorelines may have hidden dangers.

Better Monitoring Is Needed

A tsunami warning center needs to be established as soon as practical. But the occurrence of this massive and destructive tsunami does prove that megatsunamis can occur in the Indian Ocean. The Intergovernmental Oceanographic Commission should continue its efforts to develop a long-term approach to tsunami hazard mitigation through a coordinated program involving assessment, warning guidance, and mitigation aimed at at-risk communities. Improved numerical wave propagation models, new scientific studies to document paleotsunamis, and the deployment of tsunameters will help better monitor tsunami occurrences and develop inundation maps that will guide evacuation plans. As is done among Pacific nations, Indian Ocean scientists, disaster managers, policy makers, and local communities need to work together toward the common goal of creating tsunami-resistant communities with access to accurate, timely tsunami warnings. A tsunami warning center needs to be established as soon as practical in the region, and the Pacific Tsunami Warning Center should act as an interim warning center.

Many developing countries do not have the resources and will need substantial assistance. Even among nations in the Pacific rim, only three have comprehensive inundation maps, and none, including the U.S., have probabilistic tsunami flooding maps that reflect the realities of the past 30 years. Unesco's Intergovernmental Oceanographic Commission and the U.S. should help the effort in implementing the U.N.'s global tsunami hazard mitigation plan before the next Asian tsunami disaster strikes.

5

Creating an Indian Ocean Tsunami Warning System Is Futile

Keith Alverson

Keith Alverson works at the Global Ocean Observing System of the Intergovernmental Oceanographic Commission of the United Nations Educational, Scientific, and Cultural Organization, (UNESCO) where he is director of the Global Ocean Observing System (GOOS) program office.

Despite the fact that tsunamis are a historical and common occurrence, the lack of an early warning system in the Indian Ocean region led to thousands of people dying in the Indian Ocean tsunami in December 2004. The tragedy has encouraged scientists and governments to quickly act to build and implement a tsunami warning system in the area. However, a quick technological response is not the best response. Another massive tsunami in the area may not occur for decades, by which time the warning system could be dilapidated. Instead, all countries need to collaborate to create a global tsunami warning system that not only detects tsunamis but all ocean disturbances, including dangerous storm surges. The system will thus be extremely beneficial for many users, who will have a strong interest in maintaining it. Although it will be a challenge to develop a global system involving many multiple countries and scientists of

Keith Alverson, "Watching Over the World's Oceans," *Nature,* vol. 434, March 3, 2005, pp. 19–20. Copyright © 2005 by Macmillion Magazines Ltd. Reproduced by permission.

many nationalities, the life-saving results will be worth the effort.

In the mid-nineteenth century, the HMS *Beagle* docked in Concepciòn, Chile, giving [scientist] Charles Darwin the opportunity to see and describe the immediate aftermath of a tidal wave. His eyewitness account in the classic *Voyage of the Beagle* could easily be read as a report from Sri Lanka after the tsunami of 26 December 2004. The timeless nature of the devastation stands in stark contrast to the enormous progress that has occurred since then in relevant areas of science, technology and intergovernmental cooperation—progress that should have made a difference. Plate tectonics, accurate seafloor mapping, powerful computer calculations for wave propagation, real-time wireless global communications networks and operational 24-hour government warning systems are all new since Darwin's time. It seems they made no difference. With hindsight, they could have, and should have. . . .

The December tsunami was a natural catastrophe, but much of the death and destruction that followed was a result of the collective failure of human institutions. Not surprisingly, hindsight has informed the global response. In addition to the outpouring of aid, there is interest from nations wishing to build an operational tsunami warning system in the Indian Ocean as soon as possible. Although laudable, this goal is far too narrow. Why? Despite local tsunamis being a frequent occurence in the Indian basin, we have no idea when or where to expect the next large regional tsunami. It could be centuries away. A rapidly developed, single-basin, single-purpose tsunami warning system that goes unused for many years is likely to be falling apart by the time it is called to use.

This is not a wholly pessimistic view—we have been here before. Following two major tsunamis in the Pacific in the early 1960s, the Intergovernmental Oceanographic Commission (IOC) of UNESCO and its member states set up a warning system for that ocean. By 2004, the funding for the upkeep of that system was a trickle, and three of its six seafloor pressure sensors were out of commission. There has long been talk of expanding and upgrading the Pacific warning system, which lacks regional tsunami warning centres in many vulnerable areas—southeast Asia, the southwest Pacific, and Central and South America. Unfortunately, once the initial system was in place, the resources required to maintain it properly—let alone expand or improve it—were extremely difficult to find. Building a single-use warning system for the Pacific basin alone in response to the events of the early 1960s was arguably not the best thing to do. It would be a mistake for the international scientific community to suggest another quick technological fix for the Indian Ocean, where tsunamis are even less frequent.

It would be a mistake for the international scientific community to suggest another quick technological fix for the Indian Ocean.

A Multihazard Approach

A more sensible idea is to develop a global tsunami warning system that is fully integrated with an operational ocean-observing system—one that is regularly used for other related hazards, such as storm surges. Storm surges associated with tropical cyclones can hit coastal areas well ahead of the landfall of the actual storm; they travel with nearly the same rapidity as tsunamis, but occur much more frequently. And for unprepared or unwarned populations, they can be equally deadly. For example, in 1970 (and again in 1991) six- to seven-metre-high storm surges striking Bangladesh resulted in around half a million deaths. At present, there is no regional system for predicting storm surges, although there are a few national efforts. But tide gauges provide vital information for the high-resolution models used in storm-surge prediction—and these are the same data needed for tsunami warnings.

Although the scope of a tsunami warning system should be global, one of the most important components of any future network will be the national warning centres. Japan, Chile, New Zealand, Australia, French Polynesia, United States and the Russian Federation already run operational tsunami warning centres 24 hours a day, seven days a week. The track record of these centres is substantial, but it is time to improve the scope of their activities by working to build an operational, global ocean-disaster warning, preparedness and mitigation system.

In addition to detecting multiple hazards—from storm surges to cyclones—the best way to ensure that a tsunami warning system remains fully operational for decades to come is to embed it in broader efforts to observe the ocean. Data used for tsunami warnings are of potential interest to an enormous array of users and stakeholders. It is these other users who will ensure the system is maintained over the long term.

A more sensible idea is to develop a global tsunami warning system that is fully integrated with an operational ocean-observing system.

For example, changes in observed sea level occur across many timescales, from seconds and minutes (wind waves, tsunamis), hours to days (tides, storm surges), and years (seasonal cycles, El Niño), through to long-term changes associated with climate change and the movement of land masses. Ocean circulation and long-term sea-level trends are monitored by the global array of tide gauges maintained by the Global Sea Level Observing System (GLOSS) a component of the Global Ocean Observing System (GOOS). These are both run by the IOC, which aims to build a network of roughly 300 sea-level stations around the world (100 more than there are now), as well as several higher density regional networks.

Although some GLOSS stations already glean and process data in real time for the Pacific Tsunami Warning System, they operate mainly to serve the research community in a delayed mode. Upgrading the GLOSS network to real-time data delivery would contribute to a global tsunami warning system, and at the same time vastly increase its usefulness for other purposes.

For example, real-time sea-level data could contribute to ocean models serving a wide spectrum of users—including captains of large tankers who need predictions for efficient route planning. In such contexts, these data are of substantial economic interest. They can aid ship piloting in harbours, the management of sluices and barrages, tidal predictions and computations for coastal engineering design and insurance purposes.

Challenges of a Global System

There are three substantial hurdles that need to be overcome to achieve this vision. The first challenge will be to develop an operational 'real time, all the time' capability for the ocean observing system. Those components of GOOS most relevant to marine hazards, such as sea surface temperature, and sea-level and seafloor pressure, need to be made available in real time. This is not just a technical requirement, but also a difficult political issue. For example, some countries purposely limit the release of public data to monthly mean sea-level values, years after the fact, whereas their high-frequency data (1–2 minute averages) are kept private for reasons ranging from cost to national security. In addition, national centres running operationally 24 hours a day, seven days a week, are essential to a hazard warning system. With the exception of a few countries, oceanography does not have the required institutional support at the national level to enable such operations, and creative solutions will be required.

The second challenge will be to bring together the different scientific communities, such as seismologists involved in tsunami warnings, meteorologists involved in storm-surge warnings, and oceanographers involved in both, to develop an integrated, multihazard system. So far, it has been difficult to build even single-use systems except at a national level. A fully operational multihazard observing system will require unprecedented cooperation among a wide community of experts and stakeholders. But it would also dramatically improve cost-effectiveness, by both reducing the initial investment and spreading the burden of long-term costs.

The final and most difficult challenge will be to tailor the system to local cultural, social and economic conditions. Although the tsunami warning system must work on a global scale, its users will be local. As with so many things, we need to be thinking globally and acting locally. Civil populations cannot be educated or warned without accounting for—and benefiting from—local knowledge and concerns. Outreach, education and public awareness efforts will only work if they are woven into national, cultural and local environmental fabrics. For example, in Aceh, Indonesia, it has been suggested that rapid delivery of warnings could exploit the wide distribution of Islamic mosques with loudspeaker systems used for calls to prayer.

Global Thinking, Local Action

Ultimately, the development of the scientific and technical backbone of a tsunami warning system is a global responsibility, but preparedness remains a task for individual nations, or regions. This is the hardest of the three challenges and will require novel mechanisms for cooperation between scientists and social scientists, and between different organizations at the international, national and regional levels.

In particular, the international scientific community must not get carried away with the tantalizing but flawed idea that

there is a quick technological fix to these complex societal issues. Instead, we need to broker a process through which
countries of any given region come to recognize themselves as
the true owners of the system. In their eagerness to help,
states or organizations from outside the region might even
obstruct the process by which Indian Ocean rim countries
come together to plan, create and implement a system. But
such a process should develop a true sense of ownership and
responsibility. The majority of the lives lost were Asian, and
the countries of that region must be at the forefront of plans
to protect themselves in the future.

From 3 to 8 March 2005, UNESCO is hosting the first of
two technical meetings intended to foster the development of
a tsunami warning and mitigation system for the Indian
Ocean. All of the nations in the region are invited and, along
with other interested nations and international organizations,
will work together to design a comprehensive work plan and
timetable.

The challenge facing these countries, together with the
IOC and our global partners, is a substantial one. But unlike
so many visionary projects mooted by bureaucrats, the task is
both clearly defined and eminently achievable. Let us hope
that we are now taking the first step to ensure that the next
tsunami—wherever and whenever it inevitably occurs—will
not go down in history as a catastrophe, but as a tribute to
the ability of science and technology to serve society.

6

Developing Countries Lack Adequate Disaster Prevention and Recovery Programs

Suprakash Roy

Suprakash Roy is a senior professor of physics at Bose Institute in Calcutta, India.

The number of natural disasters occurring annually is on the rise and has a severe impact on the world in terms of human and economic costs. Although natural disasters are uncontrollable, the devastation which follows any natural disaster can be mitigated by humans. Countries should include disaster prevention in their development plans instead of waiting until disasters strike to provide relief. Early detection systems are helpful, but it is equally important to set up communication systems so that scientists can quickly warn government officials about impending threats. The public and government officials must also be educated to use and understand these systems once they are in place. Scientists also play an important role in natural disaster relief and in seeking ways to assist in saving human lives.

Nature's wrath is inescapable. It does not discriminate between blue and white collars, between foreign tourists in a seaside villa or local fishermen on the coast. Death by natural disasters is as old as recorded history—from the typhus epi-

Suprakash Roy, "Natural Disasters Responsibilities Should Not Cease with Donations and Relief Work," *The Statesman*, March 2, 2005. Copyright © 2005 by *The Statesman*. Reproduced by permission.

demic in Athens in 430 BC to the Shaanxi earthquake of 1556 in China, and closer home, the Bangladesh famine of 1974 and the latest tsunami that hit South-East Asia on 26 December 2004.

Even as the death toll continues to rise, it is estimated that the magnitude will surpass the number of people that were killed in Hiroshima, which was estimated to be 140,000. The difference between the two is of course, that one is natural and the other man-made, and while there is scope for preventing man-made disasters, nothing can be done to control natural disasters.

Hazard Management

The frequency of natural disasters is on the rise and has been having a more severe impact on the world in terms of human and economic cost. The reasons for increasing natural disasters, according to experts, are environmental degradation, climate change and population growth, especially in cities. While the number of lives lost has declined in the past 20 years, the number of people affected has risen. Thus, 800,000 people died from natural disasters in the 1990s compared with two million in the 1970s. However, the number of people affected by natural disasters has tripled to two billion in the last decade.

Ironically the economic losses increase as the world becomes richer and more developed. The International Red Cross Society published an annual World Disasters Report in which it was reported that, in the past two decades, direct economic losses from natural disasters has multiplied five-fold to $629 billion. In 2003 alone, there were about 700 natural disasters which killed about 75,000 people and caused about $65 billion damage. . . .

Natural disasters are uncontrollable, but the devastation which follows any natural disaster is not. Disasters are closely linked to poverty as they can wipe out decades of development in a matter of hours. More than 95 per cent of all deaths caused by disasters occur in developing countries, and losses due to natural disasters are 20 times greater (as a percent of GDP [gross domestic product]) in developing countries than in industrial countries.

Natural disasters hit poor people the hardest, and therefore, implementing effective disaster recovery programmes may be an effective means of reducing poverty. The message spread by the World Bank's Hazard Management Unit, which is working with developing countries, is to plan for potential natural hazards as a development issue instead of confronting them only as a humanitarian emergency when a crisis strikes.

Natural disasters are uncontrollable, but the devastation which follows any natural disaster is not.

At the national level, disaster prevention needs to be an integral part of a country's development plans. It is to be commended that the Indian government, under the aegis of the ministry of home affairs, has included disaster management in its development programme in the Tenth Plan.

Early Warning

After the tsunami disaster, installation of an expensive tsunami warning system in the Indian Ocean is on the way. Since many countries on the Indian Ocean coast are developing nations, what is arguably more important than a hi-tech early warning system is an improved communication system.

American scientists monitoring the Pacific had allegedly over an hour's notice of the earthquake that triggered the tsunami in the Indian Ocean, but they did not know whom to contact in these South-East Asian countries. As such, installing hi-tech instruments would be fruitless unless all countries in the region have an improved communication infrastructure in place.

A tsunami-alert system is a combination of real-time sensors, data-crunching computers and orbiting satellites, but, more important, it requires imparting training to the public and officials on how to respond to warnings. The Department of Science and Technology of the Government of India has admitted its mistake in ignoring the underwater seismic tremors near Indonesia on the grounds that the tsunami is uncommon in the Indian Ocean—however, such a costly mistake should not be repeated.

In India, about 60 per cent of the landmass is earthquake-prone, over 40 million hectares are prone to floods, eight per cent of the total area is prone to cyclones and 68 per cent of the area is susceptible to drought. It, therefore, requires taking appropriate steps to lessen the impact of nature's fury. Preventive measures and preparedness are the two basic components which can make a significant difference when it comes to protecting our development from natural hazards.

What is arguably more important than a high-tech early warning system is an improved communication system.

Developed countries have been able to reduce human and economic losses with adequate safety measures and a better response system in the aftermath of any natural tragedy. Indian and state governments are now considering the amendment of building rules in areas more prone to earthquakes. While developed countries use established insurance mechanism to reduce property losses, developing countries like India divert funds from development programmes to emergency relief and recovery.

Even without the tsunami, what India lacks is the appropriate training of personnel, awareness and maintenance of emergency equipment. Invariably when a fire breaks out in a building, the water resource meant for fighting the fire is found to be dry, or the emergency gate meant for entry of fire-engines and other emergency services is blocked by a heap of garbage. How many know how to use simple fire-fighting equipment which "decorate" offices and buildings? While developed countries routinely and religiously check all emergency systems periodically, in India they are ignored until a mishap occurs. The pattern is only too predictable—after every mishap, the inquiry committee inevitably points out the lack of proper training or negligence of duty.

Donations and Relief Are Not Enough

Tsunami is a Japanese term, meaning "harbour wave". A tsunami can be generated by any disturbance that displaces a large mass of water from its equilibrium position. Earthquakes, landslides, volcanic eruptions, explosions, and even the impact of cosmic bodies, such as meteorites, can generate tsunamis. A tsunami travels at a speed that is related to the water depth—hence, as the water depth decreases, the tsunami slows. The tsunami's energy flux, which is dependent on both its wave speed and wave height, remains nearly constant. Consequently, as the tsunami's speed diminishes as it travels into shallower water, its height grows. Because of this, a tsunami imperceptible at the middle of the sea may grow to be several metres or more in height near the coast. When it finally reaches the coast, a tsunami may appear as a rapidly rising or falling tide, a series of breaking waves. The word tsunami, which was relatively obscure and unknown in this part of the world [before the December 2004 disaster] . . . has now become part and parcel of our vocabulary and has created interest on its formation and destructive powers.

The tragic scenes . . . drive home the point that we are helpless in the hands of Mother Nature despite all our advances in science and technology. While our hearts go out to the families of the victims, we also pledge that, as scientists, our duties will not cease with donations and relief work but that we will remain constantly on the alert.

7

Developed Nations Must Help Poorer Countries Modernize

Ross Clark

Ross Clark is a writer for the London Sunday Telegraph.

Industrialization is the answer to increased survival in the event of natural disaster. Industrialized areas are more prepared to handle natural disasters through their communication infrastructures and early warning systems. However, most industrialized countries concentrate on combating the problem of global warming rather than assisting poorer countries in industrializing and thus becoming better prepared for the eventuality of disaster. For instance, many industrialized nations signed the Kyoto Treaty, agreeing to reduce the use of fossil fuel in an effort to slow global warming. However, experts estimate that the treaty will reduce global economic growth by $150 billion per year. For half this expense, Danish environmentalist Bjorn Lomborg states, the world could provide clean water, education and healthcare for everyone. Instead of focusing so single-mindedly on reducing carbon emissions, industrialized nations should help poorer ones build infrastructure such as transportation and communication systems that will aid the poor in times of disaster.

The most telling remark about last week's [December 2004] tsunamis was made by a man who was in Scandinavia when the wave struck. In response to the reported deaths of

500 of his countrymen, Goran Persson, the Swedish Prime Minister, declared: "It is probably the worst [disaster] of our time and will impact on everyday Swedish life for a long time to come."

In other words, in a country of fearsome winter storms, and where roads and railway lines are affected by ice and snow for many months of the year, the worst disaster to strike its people in living memory has occurred in a string of holiday destinations 8,000 miles away in the tropics. The point is that it isn't natural disasters which kill people, so much as poverty which prevents them protecting themselves.

It isn't natural disasters which kill people, so much as poverty which prevents them protecting themselves.

Had the tsunamis struck Scandinavia or the west coast of America, people would have died but in nothing like the numbers who died on the shores of the Indian Ocean. A flood warning system such as that employed in Britain after the catastrophic floods of 1953 would have evacuated most people to safety well in time. Communications would have been affected but whole stretches of coastline would not have been cut off for days as they were last week in Indonesia. The beaches would not still be lined with bodies nearly a week after the disaster. The affected areas would not be facing starvation and infectious disease for weeks to come.

Prosperity Saves Lives

Contrary to the many fatalistic leading articles and columns written last week, which marvelled at the awesome power of Nature and encouraged us to believe that we are entirely at her mercy, there is something countries can do to improve their chances of surviving natural disasters: namely to do everything they can to achieve prosperity and the true security that comes with it. A fully industrialised Indonesia would have had a transport system capable of getting help to the required areas. It would also have been able to react to the earthquake alerts which were issued by US seismologists hours before the disaster. At the very least it would have had a network of refrigerated mortuaries to cope with the bodies of victims without leaving them to putrefy on the beaches.

It would be fatuous to make these points were it not for the fact that the world's strategy for averting natural disasters increasingly revolves around a policy of stunting the processes of industrialisation. For the past 15 years the governments of most developed nations and most international development agencies have been preoccupied with one threat: that of steadily rising sea levels caused by global warming.

[The December 2004] tsunamis aside, almost all recent natural disasters have in some way been blamed upon global warming: the hurricanes which struck the Caribbean last summer, the heatwave that killed hundreds of Parisians in the summer of 2003, and the various famines to have struck sub-Saharan Africa over the past decade. The blame for all meteorological events, according to the doom-mongers of global warming, can be traced back to mankind's excessive burning of fossil fuels.

Moreover, according to these people, there is only one way we can hope to reduce the death toll from future disasters and that is to reduce our consumption of fossil fuels drastically. They do not deny that the policy of reducing carbon emissions will severely hamper world economic growth, only the possibility that there could be any alternative strategy for coping with the problems posed by global warming. It has been left to Bjorn Lomborg, the Danish environmentalist who has become a pariah in the scientific world, to point out that the Kyoto treaty, which commits signatory nations to sharp reductions in fossil fuel use, is extremely poor value for money. The effect of the treaty will be to reduce global economic growth by some $150 billion a year—all in the cause of postponing alleged global warming by a few years. Yet for half that sum, Lomborg calculates, the world could provide clean water, education and healthcare for all. To Lomborg, it is obvious that money would be better spent protecting vulnerable settlements from sea level rise, or rebuilding them in more elevated positions than in sacrificing economic development.

Global Warming Is Not the Problem

Yet to make this argument is to invite scorn. Global warming has become a dogma from which no dissent is to be tolerated. And so the world persists in a policy that will do little to abate global warming—such as it is—but will certainly prevent third world countries attaining the living standards of the West. The overall result will be to leave their populations more vulnerable to natural disasters.

The skewed sense of priorities shown by most Western governments was demonstrated in their response to last week's [December 2004 tsunami] disaster. Britain, which kept raising its donation towards the relief funds in line with the scale of the disaster was one of the more generous. Yet the sums are trifling compared to the money spent annually on research into global warming. Ever keen to latch on to what is important, the EU proposed a conference on disaster aid. You can bet that the sums spent feeding the delegates will dwarf the pounds 2.2 million which the EU released last week for actual disaster relief in the wake of the tsunamis.

No one is more irritated by the West's warped sense of priorities than the developing nations themselves. The Johannesburg Earth Summit in 2002 was supposed to mark the commencement of a new era of cooperation between the rich and the poor, yet it merely served to show how far they are apart. As far as the developing nations were concerned, the most important issue for discussion was that of trade. In particular, they wanted an end to the agricultural subsidies and tariff barriers that prevent them from bettering themselves by competing in our food markets. Most Western leaders, however, opted to skip these discussions, only flying in for a photo-call when the agenda had moved on to climate change.

No one is more irritated by the West's warped sense of priorities than the developing nations themselves.

If any good might come out of ... [the] tsunamis it will be to remind the world that natural disasters are just that: acts of nature that have no human cause but whose effects may be reduced by industrial development. The obsession with reducing carbon emissions will do nothing to prevent a repeat of last week's tsunamis and virtually nothing to arrest the steady rise in sea levels predicted over the next 100 years. But it will hamper the development of modern roads, airports and communication systems that could have saved tens of thousands of lives. The world's poor are being sacrificed in a misguided effort to save them.

8

Trauma Counseling Helps Disaster Victims

Sherwin B. Nuland

Sherwin B. Nuland is clinical professor of surgery at the Yale School of Medicine and a fellow of the university's Institution for Social and Policy Studies. Nuland is the author of eight books, including Doctors: The Biography of Medicine *and* The Wisdom of the Body. *He has written dozens of articles for magazines and periodicals including the* New Yorker, Time, Life, National Geographic, Discover, *the* New York Times, *and the* Los Angeles Times.

Many doctors went to countries devastated by the December 2004 tsunami to help the victims of the disaster. Some doctors discovered that the need for medical care was much different than they anticipated. In Sri Lanka the majority of victims who were badly hurt died in the disaster, leaving physicians with less work than they expected. Most of the injuries the relief doctors had to tend to were minor. However, they quickly discovered that they were still very much needed. Almost all the visiting patients exhibited psycho-physiological symptoms such as insomnia and headaches, which are physical signs of post-traumatic stress disorder. The doctors did what they could, knowing that much more would need to be done. There are only twenty trained psychiatrists in Sri Lanka, so the country will need a lot of interna-

Sherwin B. Nuland, "After the Deluge," *The New Republic,* April 11, 2005, p. 30. Copyright © 2005 by The New Republic, Inc. Reproduced by permission.

tional help to train doctors, nurses, and social workers to effectively counsel trauma patients. In addition, Sri Lanka will need help in getting people back to work quickly, as unemployment is a major source of depression. In short, there is no doubt that trauma counseling is an important facet of responding to natural disasters.

I am not sure just what it was that made me drop everything on December 31, [2004] and join six colleagues on a medical relief mission to Sri Lanka. At the moment I made the decision, it simply seemed like the right thing to do, and in retrospect it still does. But it turned out that the need for our small group was very different than we had anticipated: there was far less acute disease and injury than expected, but the human misery was of a sort that will require attention for years to come. In a strictly clinical sense, we accomplished far less than we had hoped. And yet it was important to be in that place at precisely that time. Ultimately, we did what doctors have always done, even before the Hippocratic physicians of ancient Greece enunciated their code of professional responsibility: we tried to help, as did so many others. . . .

Mostly Minor Injuries

I had brought with me a set of surgical instruments to be used as though in a field hospital, assuming that my principal work would be to treat the late consequences of major trauma. I was wrong. The tsunami had an effect similar to that of September 11, when emergency rooms all over Manhattan prepared themselves for an influx of the seriously injured, and very few came. The reason was the same: almost everyone caught up in the disaster was killed. The great majority of those who survived had minor wounds or no wounds at all. The few severely injured who somehow survived were immediately evacuated to the inadequate and dreadfully maintained hospitals that we later saw, where they were languishing dispiritedly on bare mattresses covering rusty bedsprings, amid open drainage conduits filled with fetid standing water.

My own surgical work would consist in the management of relatively minor and usually infected wounds, the great majority of which had been sustained in the days following the tsunami, during the phase of digging out, when families were seeking bodies and lost possessions. I saw at least half my patients while functioning as what might be called a family physician, much as my five colleagues were doing. The refugees who came to us, apathetic and worn down by a chronicity of poverty and despair to which the tsunami had added a magnum of hopelessness, lined up because they needed to see, or wanted to see, a doctor, for any of several reasons. Sometimes those reasons would prove to be related to the most recent disaster in minimal or unexpected ways, as would be impressed on us again and again in our travels from camp to camp.

A warm smile and an arm around the shoulder probably did more for most of our patients than the medications that we gave them for the various complaints.

We soon discovered that the real good we were doing was not what we had expected it to be. It was not medical need, strictly speaking, that made our presence so important to the families in these crushed places to which we had come from half a world away. It was our physical presence that counted. A warm smile and an arm around the shoulder probably did more for most of our patients than the medications that we gave them for the various complaints so often unaccompanied by any physical findings that might account for them. It was the touching of a hand, the lingering of a man or woman's hand in my own, that seemed to mean so much, or the unexpected hug that made a frightened child laugh in surprise. Comparing notes at the end of our first day, we realized that we were dealing far less with physical than with psychological wounds and inflammations.

The prevailing mood of our patients—virtually all of whom had been living a bare pre-tsunami subsistence on the yields of fishing or the milk derived from the spavined cows and goats that roamed every byway and street to graze on garbage and similar detritus—was a kind of resigned lethargy. Except in a few instances, we never saw sorrow or any evidence of grieving, despite the reality that so many had lost loved ones, and all had lost their homes and everything they owned. There must have been plenty of widows and widowers and orphans among our patients, but no detached observer could tell which of these dispirited people they were. All of this contrasted remarkably with the general atmosphere of Batticaloa itself, where people in the shops and the streets were going about their business seemingly unaffected by the horrific events that had taken place so close to them.

A Depressed Society

The members of our team, came from a variety of professional backgrounds and specialties, and who ranged in age from late twenties to early seventies, were in agreement that the repressed mourning that soon became so obvious was manifesting itself in symptoms that could arise only from that very suppression of overt emotional response. Physicians call such symptoms psycho-physiological. They typically consist of the assortment of complaints that I would hear over and over as our interpreters struggled to make English sense of what they were being told: "I shake a lot now"; "I can't feel my arms and legs anymore"; "I have an itching inside my chest"; "My belly is swollen"; "I have headaches all the time"; "I can't sleep." All these reports of inner states were without any objective findings associated with them, as was the too-frequent abdominal pain, or the invisible rash insistently described to me and my incredulous interpreter by one middle-aged man.

In any culture in the world, including those that are reputed to have the ability to face hardship and loss with a religious serenity, these are worrisome complaints, because they tell a physician that rage, guilt, conflict, or any of several other unhappy and unwelcome emotional states are being converted into symptomatology that is mistakenly attributed to organic causes. Of course, there were some dehydrated children who needed treatment, and the occasional respiratory or middle ear infection or relatively mild diarrhea as well as a variety of other minor illnesses and that assortment of infected wounds that I cleaned and dressed—but all of us agreed that we were witnessing an alarming phenomenon, the kind of situation that too frequently foretells later overt psychological breakdown.

The danger lies in the ... widespread manifestations of the condition known as post-traumatic stress disorder.

It was not enough that we were observing these warnings in so many individuals. The greater concern was that a society that has suddenly lost more than 35,000 souls and an untold number of homes, a society filled with bereft and haunted adults and children who have not only lost so much but have also seen so much, a society of which so many members were impoverished and without hope long before the tsunami— this is a society in danger. The danger lies in the virtual inevitability in the months to come of widespread manifestations of the condition known as post-traumatic stress disorder, in essence a serious form of depression recognized under various names for more than a century in survivors of major calamities, but only in recent decades fully described in all of its perilous characteristics. No matter how individuals may suffer, an even greater danger is a kind of national inertia, loss of productivity, and an inability to deal with the realities of everyday life.

With each passing day of our mission, increasing numbers of NGOs [nongovernmental organizations] and the larger agencies arrived to provide medical aid, until it seemed that we were all getting in one another's way. Before long, our small group became not only redundant but less effective than we had been at first. It became clear that, having obtained a microcosmic perception by our work in the camps, the best way to contribute something of macrocosmic and perhaps lasting significance was to make observations in the devastated areas, to speak at some length to survivors of the tsunami, and then—utilizing the knowledge of the members of our team with wide experience in Third World countries—to make recommendations to . . . any representatives of the Sri Lankan government who might wish to speak with us. As it turned out, these included the prime minister and the minister of health; but we soon came to realize that . . . our other contacts seemed too concerned with the immediate problems (or perhaps with impressing upon us how well they were dealing with their country's fragility) to focus on matters that might become troublesome as the months wore on.

A Need for Counselors

Of greatest concern is the significant probability—several of our number, myself included, consider it a virtual inevitability—of what might be called a national epidemic of posttraumatic stress disorder involving large segments of the populations directly or indirectly affected by the tsunami. There are only twenty trained psychiatrists in the entire country, so a great deal of help will be needed, especially skilled professionals to train physicians, nurses, men and women who work in social services. Many will be required in order to provide psychological counseling and various forms of support. For the heartbreaking number of children who have been left without parents, the country must have a complete overhaul of its orphanages and a critical evaluation of its adoption procedures.But Sri Lanka will need far more than attention to the havoc caused by the tsunami itself. There is an absolute necessity to put people back to work—so soon, indeed, that it must be thought of as an emergency measure. As is true of so many Third World countries, this is a chronically depressed society in which large numbers of men and women are barely or not at all occupied in meaningful work. Upon this long-standing problem has been thrown the acute and immense psychological burden of enormous loss, displacement, and an exacerbation of underlying mistrust of the government, as well as a certain overt denial of the emotional effects of the tragedy, as manifest in ordinary behavior. To illustrate the prevalence of chronic clinical depression predating the tragedy, the national suicide rate is said to be so high that the major hospital in Batticaloa (and elsewhere as well, we were told) has a poison intensive care unit, because villagers and others so often try to do away with themselves by ingesting fertilizers and insecticides, the only sufficiently toxic materials available to the poor.

A Country with Much to Do

The urgent necessity to put people to work dovetails with the country's most important long-term need, which is a national undertaking to rebuild a woefully inadequate and even dangerous infrastructure of roads, bridges, hospitals, and dwelling places. Supplies and equipment have poured into the country since the tsunami, but transportation between parts of the island is so difficult that this, far more than any lack of materials, has been a major factor standing in the way of aid and recovery efforts. As part of achieving these goals, the entire hospital system must be rebuilt. Not only are the conditions for patients and staff appalling, but the very architecture of Sri Lanka stands in the way of effective care. The major hospitals are built in the antiquated pavilion style, the former colonial model long discarded for modern facilities because of its inefficiency and its difficulty to maintain.

As two of my medical teammates—an internist and an infectious-disease expert who have been involved in disaster relief in such places as East Timor, Kosovo, Chechnya, and several African countries—pointed out, there is no single international organization capable of responding immediately with massive aid and the ability to coordinate the efforts of the many NGOs and individual groups that begin to pour in once they have overcome the logistical problems of getting themselves under way. The huge outfits such as the Red Cross and the United Nations take too long to arrive in full force and seem far less systematized than one is led to believe. What is needed is an international working conference on disaster relief that brings together all the appropriate experts and groups, and coordinates a predictably functional system that is reviewed each year. What better place to hold such a conference than Colombo?

There are only twenty trained psychiatrists in the entire country, so a great deal of help will be needed.

Sri Lanka needs a re-orientation of its national priorities. Its location and its extraordinary natural beauty have gifted the island nation with the potential to build one of the leading tourist industries in Asia—yet it has remained barely developed, largely because of poor infrastructure, little investment, sparseness of know-how, and a seeming inability to recognize possibilities. And there is the terrifying political context for all the island's miseries: the decades-long excruciation of an ethnic and religious war in which 64,000 people have so far been killed. (It was in this savage conflict that suicide bombing was invented as an instrument of war.) An outburst of economic accomplishment, with its accompanying improvement of conditions across the social and ethnic divisions within the country, would go a long way toward healing some of the open wounds that have served to perpetuate the

Tamil rebellion and to frustrate the thus far inadequate internal and international efforts to solve it. The key to all this will very likely prove to be far less the role of the Sri Lankan government than the participation of its private internal organizations and the international business community.

Is there what Americans would call an "upside" to such a catastrophe? In the wake of such massive and arbitrary suffering, the search for a saving significance is inescapable. And so it is important to remember that success breeds success, and spreads its effects among the disaffected and rebellious as it spreads optimism, a sense of goodwill, and the capacity to compromise in order to perpetuate gains that are being made. By bringing the world's attention to the acute and chronic disasters of Sri Lanka, the tsunami may paradoxically have come with the silver lining that lifts the country, and some of the other involved areas, out of its long-standing state of neglect and torpor and despair.

9

Trauma Counseling May Not Help Victims

Erzulie Coquillon

Erzulie Coquillon is a master's student in counseling psychology at Boston College and is a member of the Ignacio Martín-Baró Fund for Mental Health and Human Rights.

Mental health experts believe that nine out of ten survivors of the December 2004 tsunami are likely to experience some sort of post-traumatic stress. Some of these experts argue that without therapy, the survivors will suffer from long-term emotional problems with devastating consequences and that foreign aid should therefore include crisis counseling. In fact, psychological help from outsiders is usually not helpful and may be especially ineffective in war-torn Sri Lanka, which is just emerging from a civil war. Sri Lankans have complicated emotional needs because of the past traumas they have experienced during their war. In order to assist Sri Lankans with their psychological needs, counselors must understand the people's culture and complex past—an understanding usually only native healers possess. Understanding this, the Sri Lankan government has asked that international donors provide food and medical supplies rather than psychological aid.

Erzulie Coquillon, "Post-Tsunami Psychosocial Relief Efforts in Sri Lanka," *The Just Word,* Spring 2005, pp. 1–2. Copyright © 2005 by the Ignacio Martín-Baró Fund for Mental Health and Human Rights. Reproduced by permission.

The tsunami that devastated parts of Sri Lanka, Indonesia, Thailand, India, the Maldives, and Africa on December 26, 2004 was the worst in 40 years. The death toll is estimated at 250,000 and the number of displaced persons far larger. Indonesia and Sri Lanka were hardest hit; on the western tip of the Indonesian island of Sumatra, the closest inhabited area to the epicenter of the earthquake, more than 70% of the inhabitants of some coastal villages are reported dead. In Sri Lanka, at least 31,000 people are confirmed dead, thousands are missing, and up to one million people are homeless.

Psychological Aid Is Complicated

In a recent conference in Bangkok, mental health experts estimated that up to nine in ten survivors of the tsunami are likely to suffer from psychological trauma, and the mental health damage could last years. Somchai Chakrabhand, head of Thailand's Mental Health Department, said that "about 30% of people in tsunami-hit areas showed signs of moderate post-traumatic stress disorder, such as being unable to sleep or look at the sea. Another 20% were 'very significantly affected,' he added, 'displaying symptoms such as an obsession with waiting for the return of their loved ones [according to a BBC News report on February 2, 2005].'" "Without the necessary help . . . the long-term effects could be as devastating as the tsunami itself," Chakrabhand told the BBC. Yet, as we suggest here, this is only a "partial story."

Counseling Offers Minimal Help

Psychosocial workers in crisis situations argue that individual and small group psychotherapy is limited in its ability to address the myriad social and communal implications of disaster or war, including the rupture of social relations and institutions, the fracturing of communities, and the shifting roles of survivors. Moreover, they acknowledge that recognition and affirmation of local survivors' skills, traditions, and practices fosters survivors' psychological healing in the initial phases of reconstruction and lays the groundwork for long-term development. Indeed, the Sri Lankan government, reflecting this awareness, expressed a preference for food and medical supplies from international donors rather than psychological aid.

In January [2005], Dr. Athula Sumathipala, chief of the psychosocial desk at the Sri Lankan government's Center for National Operations, told *The New York Times* that "We believe the most important thing is to strengthen local coping mechanisms rather than imposing counseling." This sentiment, which has been echoed by Western researchers . . . is reflected in the words of [psychologist] Ignacio Martín-Baró when he wrote about the foundation for a people's mental health lying ". . . in the existence of humanizing relationships, of collective ties within which and through which the personal humanity of each individual is acknowledged and in which no one's reality is denied" arguing further that "the building of a new society, or at least a better and more just society, is not only an economic and social problem; it is essentially a mental health problem."

We believe the most important thing is to strengthen local coping mechanisms rather than imposing counseling.

These concerns are especially relevant for Sri Lanka, which only recently emerged from prolonged civil war. Sri Lanka is a small, ethnically and religiously diverse nation; Ceylon and Indian Tamils make up about 17% of the country's population, and 74% of the population is Sinhalese. Most Sinhalese are Buddhist; most Tamils are Hindu; the 1978 Sri Lankan constitution, while assuring freedom of religion, grants primacy to Buddhism. For more than 20 years a civil war between the Sri Lankan government and Tamil separatists known as the LTTE or Tamil Tigers destabilized Sri Lanka; while a cease fire is now in place, fears of a resurgence remain. . . .

Aid Agencies Should Work with Local Healers

Many survivors of the tsunami in Sri Lanka are attempting to navigate this legacy of conflict and a threat of its renewal as well as the natural disaster. For those who have lived for years with the memories of those "disappeared" at the hands of LTTE or government forces, the disappearance of a loved one as a result of natural disaster takes on new dimensions. For some, the disturbance of ritual and the absence of a corpse to confirm a loved one's death can suspend or freeze the grieving process. In addition, the natural disaster may have disturbed or destroyed communal spaces such as temples and schools in which survivors of tragedy mourn the dead, make meaning of their losses, and reconnect to the social network, rituals, and traditions from which they draw personal meaning and identity.

When counseling is appropriate in such contexts, it is best done in conjunction with indigenous healers.

Aid workers are challenged to address the complex stressors experienced by survivors with an awareness of the impact of a history of conflict and the legacies of poverty on the population. Successful efforts will also be grounded in community needs and facilitate community members capacities to deliver resources—local as well as those provided by the international community—within their cultural context in order to secure stable, long-term rehabilitation. Thus, when counseling is appropriate in such contexts, it is best done in conjunction with indigenous healers, with an emphasis on the individual or group's survival of the crisis, rather than on perceived pathology. The Sri Lankan government has made public recommendations aimed at discouraging foreign counseling services working independently of local agencies post-tsunami and encouraging research that is beneficial to the local community.

10

The U.S. Government's Response to Disasters Discriminates Against the Poor and Minorities

Ted Steinberg

Ted Steinberg is a professor of history and law at Case Western Reserve University and is the author of Acts of God: The Unnatural History of Natural Disaster in America, Nature Incorporated: Industrialization and the Waters of New England *and* Down to Earth: Nature's Role in American History.

The flooding of Hannibal, Missouri, in 1993 only affected those who lived in the more affordable flood plains. A recently built levee protected the middle- and upper-class heart of the town, but the city's decision to spend less money on a smaller levee left the poorer residents' homes unprotected from flooding and under eight feet of water. After the disaster, the city newspaper implied that the flood was an inevitable "act of God." However, it was not inevitable that the poorer residents of Hannibal suffered most from the flooding. The government and the media routinely describe natural disasters as unavoidable forces of nature or God as a way to justify policies that protect those with more economic and political power while discriminating against the poor and minorities.

In Hannibal, Missouri—Hometown, U.S.A.—Mark Twain means big business. Nineteen ninety-six brought over 600,000 camera-toting tourists to the village that defines the sentimentalized picture of nineteenth-century life and culture envisioned by so many Americans. They come to visit the famed author's boyhood home, lunch at the Mark Twain Dinette, wander Main Street, pose before the most famous picket fence in history, and, above all, indulge themselves in a fantasy of whitewashed Americana. Hannibal can seem like a huge Norman Rockwell painting come to life.

But venture beyond the kitsch of this commodified hometown and you will find a darker, more problematic picture. The problems begin with the Mississippi River, the 2,000-mile-long father of waters that Twain navigated as a riverboat captain and immortalized in prose. Floods have long been a part of life in Hannibal. The first major flood on record occurred back in 1851, when Twain was still a town resident. In the recent past, however, the problem of flooding has worsened considerably. Of the ten most severe inundations in the city's history—as measured by the depth of the Mississippi—nine have occurred since 1960. Needless to say, the thought of 5,000 tons of water inside a historic residence such as Mark Twain's house—the city's central tourist attraction—could make any curator nervous.

Flood Precautions

In 1985, the U.S. Army Corps of Engineers figured out a way to safe guard the Twain home and the rest of Hannibal's historic area. It would build a 3,000-foot floodwall that would stretch from the Mark Twain Memorial Bridge all the way to Bear Creek, slightly south of downtown. When it was finished, the wall stood 12 feet high and surrounded the city like a fort. It cost $8 million to construct, and of that amount the corps paid the vast majority; the city contributed the remainder, mostly by donating land for the project. In 1990, ground was broken. Three years later, in the spring of 1993, Hannibal's wall stood completed—and not a moment too soon.

The structure was designed to withstand a 500-year flood, an event with just a fraction of a chance of happening in any given year. No one could have imagined that such an incredibly rare deluge would wind up baptizing the floodwall only a month after its completion. In this respect, the wall gave new meaning to the word *timely*. The Mississippi crested at nearly 32 feet, almost double flood-stage at Hannibal, making the 1993 flood far and away the worst in the city's history. "You can see how an event like this would cause the penning of the Bible," said city engineer Bob Williamson. Yet despite all the water, the floodwall worked, and Hannibal's downtown remained dry.

The traditional response to natural disaster does not benefit everyone equally.

Environmentalists have long argued that the building of levees and walls has actually contributed to the destructiveness of floods. Although these structures offer short-term protection, when erected on both sides of a stream they force the water level to rise during heavy rain (instead of simply spreading out over the floodplain), causing it to surge over the top of the levee and punishing the "protected" area with all the more force. But in this instance, at least, the corps stood vindicated, and the agency pointed to its success as evidence of the effectiveness of the structural response to floods. Build a wall high and wide enough and it may well succeed in engineering a city out of harm's way.

Flooding the Poor

For Hannibal's poor, however, the 1993 flood demonstrated a rather different lesson: that the traditional response to natural disaster does not benefit everyone equally. Back in 1962, when the corps was first asked by the city to intervene in its flood woes, the agency had proposed a much longer, more equitable wall. That project would have protected the downtown *and* the city's poorer sections—the South Side and Bear Creek Bottom. But the plan was shelved in 1965 after Hannibal officials failed to muster sufficient support for it; residents objected both to its cost to the city and to its aesthetic effects. Then, in 1973, a flood so devastating that it turned Main Street into a marina inspired city leaders to ask the corps to dust off the old floodwall plan. In rekindling their support for federal intervention, however, they made clear that they were no longer interested in the corps' initial proposal. They wanted instead a more budget-oriented, not to mention class-conscious structure—one that would save Mark Twain's old home and the rest of the downtown, but without the added expense of protecting the city's poor.

Predictably, Hannibal's poorest residents were drenched in almost eight feet of water in 1993, leading some victims to question the city's approach to flood control. One South Side resident, Virginia Foiles, expressed frustration at the protection offered Twain's home, while her own was left to rot underwater. "They put in a floodwall to save Mark Twain's house and all the stuff about that dead man, so I don't know why they don't help the living," she said. "Hannibal is for Mark Twain and Mark Twain only," lamented Donna Pagett, also of the South Side. "They could care less about their people." In the Midwest, in contrast to the East and West coasts, it is often the poor who wind up living in the floodplains, a point made by another Hannibalian, Shellia Todd. "We can't afford to live anywhere else but down here where it floods," she remarked. "It's always the poor people that get screwed."

Not an Act of God

Twain, with his proclivity for social protest, would have been appalled. Not only had Hannibal's boosters transformed him

69

into a commodity (and a rather sanitized one at that); they had shored up the value of their investment with a structure emphatic in its articulation of class power. "We realize that the floodwall does not protect everyone, and that is indeed regrettable," explained Twain's hometown paper, the *Courier-Post*. "But wherever a line is drawn, someone always will be just on the wrong side of it." There are indeed always winners and losers in the struggle to combat natural disaster, this much is true. But there is nothing natural or inevitable about this fact, as the paper seemed to imply. Hannibal's trial by flood was certainly no act of God. . . .

Natural disasters, explains geographer Kenneth Hewitt, are often seen—even by those charged with studying them—as resulting chiefly from chance, "natural extremes, modified in detail but fortuitously by human circumstances." According to the dominant view of natural calamity, as outlined by Hewitt, these events are understood by scientists, the media, and technocrats as primarily accidents—unexpected, unpredictable happenings that are the price of doing business on this planet. Seen as freak events cut off from people's everyday interactions with the environment, they are positioned outside the moral compass of our culture. As a result, no one can be held accountable for them.

Taking Responsibility

This constrained vision of responsibility, this belief that such disasters stem solely from random natural forces, is tantamount to saying that they lie entirely outside human history, beyond our influence, beyond moral reason, beyond control. In truth, however, natural calamities frequently do not just happen; they are produced through a chain of human choices and natural occurrences, and in this sense they form a legitimate topic for social and historical study. Thus we should begin by considering how the inert view of the "natural" disaster came to be, how it eclipsed the idea that God had brought forth calamity in response to the evil deeds of the people themselves. Whose interests has this aseptic, natural understanding of calamity served? I argue that the tendency to see nature as the real culprit emerged in the late nineteenth century but not, as one might expect, because of better scientific knowledge (though this trend clearly played an important role later). Rather, the concept of "natural" disaster developed when those in power in disaster-stricken cities sought to normalize calamity in their quest to restore order, that is, to restore property values and the economy to their upward trajectory.

The official response to natural disaster is profoundly dysfunctional.

The emphasis on chaotic nature as the culprit—to the exclusion of human economic forces—has in this country influenced not just the local response to disaster, but the entire federal strategy for dealing with the problem. Centered largely on prediction and control, the U.S. government's approach has been overwhelmingly scientific and technological in orientation. The careful monitoring of the nation's atmosphere, rivers, and geological formations; the building of levees and floodwalls; the introduction of cloud seeding—these are just a few examples of how attempts to predict and control nature have remained at the heart of the nation's policy response. Few would dispute that there can be positive gains from such measures. But as [researcher of economic development] J.M. Albala-Bertrand has noted, natural disasters are not simply technical matters in need of more and better engineering; they are at their core sociopolitical issues. The present constellation of responses has not benefited everyone equally, as the Hannibal case demonstrates. Worse still, by recruiting an angry God or chaotic nature to their cause, those in power have been able to rationalize the economic choices that help to explain

71

why the poor and people of color—who have largely borne the brunt of these disasters—tend to wind up in harm's way. The official response to natural disaster is profoundly dysfunctional in the sense that it has both contributed to a continuing cycle of death and destruction and also normalized the injustices of class and race. . . .

Blaming God

When one reflects on the array of human forces that conspired to cause disaster along the Mississippi in 1993—the corps' construction of floodwalls, the government-sponsored levee building and farming that has led to the disappearance, for example, of over 80 percent of Missouri's wetlands—it may surprise some to learn that almost one in five Americans saw the deluge as an act of God. According to a Gallup poll, 18 percent of those surveyed agreed with the following statement: "The recent floods in the Midwest are an indication of God's judgment on the people of the United States for their sinful ways."

Seeing floods, earthquakes, and storms as signs of God's displeasure is arguably one of the oldest ways of interpreting these events. Consider, for example, the words of Minister Thomas Foxcroft, writing in the aftermath of the 1727 earthquake that struck New England, a fairly intense shock felt over 75,000 square miles. Foxcroft saw the event as evidence of God's "divine power." Yet he also understood the earthquake as "a Token of *Wrath* kindled against a Place for the Wickedness of them that dwell therein." For the colonists, what we now call natural disasters were events heavily laden with moral meaning. They were morality tales that the God-fearing told to one another.

Foxcroft and his flock lived in a world where nothing happened at random. It was a world ruled, explains historian Donald Hall, by "radical contingency." Events such as earthquakes and floods always carried a larger, deeper meaning as manifestations of God's will. Another historian, Maxine Van de Wetering, has examined sermons written after the 1727 and 1755 New England earthquakes, the latter centered east of Cape Ann, Massachusetts, and felt over some 300,000 square miles. All the texts agreed that a "moral imbalance in human behavior" had caused the ground to shake. For these ministers, de Wetering concludes, "earthquakes, especially tragic ones, were not merely luckless occasions for the chance sufferer; they were deeply meaningful punishments and conspicuous warnings."

Drawing Moral Lessons

Indeed, the tendency to derive moral lessons from geophysical extremes remained a strong current in American religious thought into the nineteenth century. When three massive earthquakes occurred along Missouri's New Madrid fault in 1811 and early 1812—unrivaled in the continental United States in severity and scope—they were interpreted by many as a sign of God's power. They also seem to have inspired those who had somehow lost their faith in God to return to the fold. [Scholar] James Lal Penick notes that in the midwestern and southern states, where the quakes were felt most forcefully, membership in the Methodist church increased from 30,741 in 1811, to 45,983 in 1812. That was a stunning increase, especially when one considers that Methodist membership rose by only 1 percent in the rest of the country. Many citizens of the young republic, explains Penick, sought moral lessons in natural calamities, viewing such phenomena as signs and portents.

Today, if one believes the pollsters, only about one-fifth of Americans derive such moral lessons from extremes of nature. What the remaining population thinks on the matter is unclear. Many no doubt see natural disasters as simple acts of nature, a view that reflects the increasing secularization of twentieth-century American society. To most people these events probably lack any clear moral imperative or lesson. Natural calamity has become, if you will, demoralized, except of course in the sharply confined circles of the superfaithful.

This trend toward demoralization was given a boost by the state's increasing role in rationalizing disaster. Especially in the years after the Second World War, the long arm and deep pockets of the federal government assumed an ever greater share of the costs associated with natural calamities. The government provided money to repair public facilities; it funded emergency housing and offered loans; it later paid to remove debris from private property, distributed food coupons, and, beginning in 1968, provided national flood insurance. For the most part, these changes helped to underwrite increasing development in hazardous areas. But just as important, they also worked to sever risk from space. In other words, disasters were no longer simply acute local problems. Instead, the risk associated with living in, say, a flood- or earthquake prone area was now amortized to taxpayers across the country. And when the risk of disaster was detached from the space in which it occurred, it became much harder to point the finger of blame. Ethical responsibility, not to mention ecological literacy, suffered in a world where everyone and thus no one bore the cost of residing in a hazard zone.

Poor Minorities Suffer

It is also clear that the demoralization of calamity has resulted in a new set of rhetorical opportunities for those in power. Once, the idea of invoking God in response to calamity was a strategy for eliciting moral responsibility. In the twentieth century, however, calling out God's name amounted to an abdication of moral reason. With the religiously inclined less disposed than ever to take acts of God seriously, the opportunity has arisen over the last century for some public officials to employ God-fearing language as a way—thinly veiled though it may be—of denying their own culpability for calamity. In this sense, the act of God concept has become little more than a convenient evasion.

The act of God concept has become little more than a convenient evasion.

Natural disasters have come to be seen as random, morally inert phenomena—chance events that lie beyond the control of human beings. In short, the emphasis has been on making nature the villain. When Hurricane Hugo swept over the South Carolina coast in 1989, for example, *Time* proclaimed in its headline that the "Winds of Chaos" had arrived, citing a wind speed of 150 miles per hour. Most news reports used a slightly lower number, at landfall, of 135 mph. Yet according to civil engineer Peter Sparks of Clemson University, the sustained winds were actually in the neighborhood of 90 to 95 mph (*gusts* were in the 100 to 130 mph range). Surely there is a connection between the effort to puff up nature's fury, and thus naturalize the disaster, and the fact that even five years after the storm virtually no action had occurred on updating building codes throughout South Carolina. It turns out that since the early 1960s engineers have known about the need for proper wind-loading criteria when building in hurricane-prone locales. But that standard has been largely ignored out of respect for development interests, explaining why Hugo was so destructive even though it was nowhere near the mega-hurricane that the media made it out to be.

The next time the wind kicks up and the earth starts to roar, what will we tell ourselves? Will we rise up in indignation at what nature has done to us? Or will we reflect on our own role as architects of destruction? It is how we answer these questions that will determine the future of calamity.

11

Nations Should Provide Aid for Humanitarian Reasons Alone

The Economist

Although disaster aid should be a selfless response of all countries after a catastrophe, the 2004 Asian tsunami proved that aid could easily be used for political gain. Tony Blair, the British prime minister pledged to give more aid in order to seem more generous and to win votes from British constituents. Bickering between countries about who had given more and who was not giving enough soon erupted as well. The American government donated relief funds hoping that it would prove the country's generosity to Muslims and help to quell terrorism. It seemed that no governments were giving relief aid simply for the sake of helping victims. Worse, some of the promised aid may never materialize. Countries that experienced natural disasters in the last decade are still awaiting relief pledged to help them recover. Instead of focusing on disaster aid for political reasons, it would be more helpful if governments would donate funds to help poor countries develop the infrastructure and warning systems that would reduce casualties and the damage caused by natural disasters.

Disaster aid is generally thought to be different: everyone is for it. Development aid, by contrast, is often overtly political (it tends to go to friends) and always controversial (is it squandered? does it breed dependency?). Humanitarian aid given after, or during, wars is almost as contentious: it may be used by one side or the other to keep the fighting going or, by donors, to influence the outcome. But aid given after a natural disaster is pure, an affirmation of the best of the human spirit, uncontaminated by politics. That's what used to be said, anyway. It is the first piece of received wisdom to deserve examination after Asia's catastrophe.

Thus came the first politicisation of the tsunami aid: governments using it to win votes at home.

Response for the Wrong Reasons

Not that individuals have failed to respond generously to the disaster [the 2004 tsunami in the Indian Ocean], quite the opposite. They reached for their credit cards from the start, leaving governments scrambling to show themselves just as big-hearted. [British prime minister] Tony Blair promised on January 5th [2005] to outdo, with British taxpayers' money, whatever they might contribute voluntarily as individuals. Thus came the first politicisation of the tsunami aid: governments using it to win votes at home.

Then came the use of aid to score old points. Jan Egeland, the United Nations' emergency-relief co-ordinator, was accused of being churlish towards the Americans by calling western countries' first pledges stingy; and the French and some other Europeans, joined by some senior UN officials, were cross that the United States had at first set up a "regional core group" with Japan, India and Australia, but not with the European Union or any European country. On January 6th [2005] Colin Powell, America's secretary of state, announced at a tsunami-relief summit in Jakarta that the group would be disbanded, and many of its assets would be put under UN direction.

By this time the aid issue was being used to peddle some pet schemes. Gordon Brown, Britain's finance minister, was arguing the case for a debt moratorium for the countries worst affected. Debt is a crippling burden for many countries, especially in Africa, but relieving it may not be the wisest way to help a government, like Indonesia's, that chooses to spend 3% of its GDP on defence but only 1.3% on education and 0.6% on health. . . .

Some people, however, have much grander, even more political, aims for aid-giving. Mr Powell spelled out his in Indonesia before the summit: "We'd be doing it regardless of religion," he said of America's contribution. "But I think it does give the Muslim world . . . an opportunity to see American generosity, American values in action. . . . And I hope that, as a result of our efforts, as a result of our helicopter pilots being seen by the citizens of Indonesia helping them, that value system of ours will be reinforced." American aid helped dry up the "pools of dissatisfaction" that led to terrorism, he said. But in Aceh, where Indonesian Islamist groups are giving relief, some Muslims have denounced America's help as cynically motivated.

Is the Response Enough?

Never mind the motives: is the aid doing any good? By this week, the main concerns were to prevent epidemics, especially those caused by dirty water, to find and tend the injured, to provide shelter and start clearing the debris. Children, who made up over a third of the tsunami's victims, according to the UN Children's Fund, are a key concern. With more money pledged in the week to January 3rd than the UN had received in the whole of 2004, cash is not the problem. Getting aid workers in place and providing the millions of displaced people with food, shelter, clean water and medical help are much harder.

The aid issue was being used to peddle some pet schemes.

Outsiders' relief operations fall into two categories. First, some foreign governments have sent members of their armed forces. The United States has dispatched more than 20 naval ships, including an aircraft carrier, the USS *Abraham Lincoln*, and a hospital ship, plus 1,300 marines. It has also sent six big transport aircraft and nine surveillance and rescue planes. Britain has sent two naval vessels; military help has also come from Australia, Germany and Pakistan. Japan is planning military aid.

Meanwhile, umpteen aid agencies have joined the cause. More than 50, said the UN, were this week opening field hospitals in Aceh alone, and countless more are working in other stricken places. Many were present in one of four regional centres: Colombo, Sri Lanka's capital; Banda Aceh, the provincial capital of Aceh; Meulaboh, not far to its south; and U-Tapao, a military base in Thailand.

But who was in charge? No one. At the summit in Jakarta, a powerful array of world leaders pledged to put their contributions through the UN; until then, only rough co-ordination efforts had been carried out by its agencies and the American-powered "regional core group".

Aid for Redevelopment

Prior to the meeting, Mr Egeland was still appealing for more help, especially for helicopters, fork-lift trucks, boats, planes, air-traffic-control units and lorries. The International Federation of Red Cross and Red Crescent Societies says half a million people will need emergency help for another six months. Then, though, as reconstruction begins, the disaster relief will start turning into development aid. What can the victims, and their governments, expect?

Disappointment, if past form is repeated. Of the $1.1 billion pledged to help the people of the Iranian city of Bam, destroyed by an earthquake in 2003, only $17.5m was sent, according to the Iranian government. Mozambique likewise received less than half of the $400m it was promised after the floods of 2000, said a minister. And Honduras and Nicaragua still await two-thirds of the $8.7 billion proffered after Hurricane Mitch swept through in 1998. Other countries have similar tales to tell. The IMF [International Monetary Fund], World Bank and individual countries accused of breaking their word may have had good reasons for doing so: perhaps the intended recipients were in no position to make good use of further money. But, if so, donors should now be more careful about their pledges.

There are other fears: that "aid fatigue" will set in, leading donors to forget other needy recipients, such as AIDS and malaria sufferers, and the people of Africa. That would be tragic, and an insult to countries like India, whose prime minister was, despite the devastation in Tamil Nadu and elsewhere, going ahead with a long-scheduled AIDS meeting this week.

Many poor countries are already concerned that the lofty aims adopted by 191 countries in the UN Millennium Declaration may be in jeopardy. One prominent aim was for rich countries to strive to reach the long-standing objective of giving 0.7% of GDP to development aid. Several of the countries that have been loudest in their declarations of generosity in the past fortnight are laggards in the giving of development aid. Germany provides just 0.28% of GDP, Britain 0.34%, France 0.41%. The United States, though its citizens are individually generous, is at the bottom of the rich countries' table, giving 0.15% of GDP.

Learning from Experience

Hopes and fears, however, do not rest on cash alone. If good is to come of the disaster it will come of wider lessons learned. The lateness of the response, the lack of an early-warning system, the paucity of rapid-reaction units and the absence of an overall relief co-ordinator all demand solutions. At present the United States is the only power with a worldwide reach but, even so, it took six days to get 40 helicopters to work in the disaster areas. The UN, for its part, has more experience than any other organisation in delivering emergency relief, but it is a sprawling group of agencies with no resources worth speaking of other than those of its member countries. Somehow power and experience must be married and, with the help of the EU, Japan and others, persuaded to set up a standing disaster-response unit that can act at short notice.

Lastly, more thought, and aid, must be given to reducing the cost and casualties caused by natural disasters. The numbers affected in such catastrophes have been rising dramatically in recent years and, according to a report by a charity, Tearfund, they are mostly in poor countries. Tearfund points to the effectiveness of such measures as planting trees to reduce the impact of floods and landslides, building techniques to help houses withstand earthquakes, cyclone shelters, sea dykes and so on. The United States Geological Survey reckons that the economic losses from natural disasters in the 1990s could have been reduced by $280 billion by investing just one-seventh of that sum in such measures. But giving for such ends is not fashionable. Six months before Mozambique was inundated in 2000, its government appealed for $2.7m to prepare for an emergency. It received less than half that. After the floods, but only after them, donors gave about $200m.

As it happens, a UN conference on disaster-reduction has long been planned to take place in the Japanese city of Kobe from January 18th to 22nd. May it lead to action, as well as words.

12

Developers Should Build More Carefully on Coastlines

David M. Bush, William J. Neal, and Robert S. Young

David M. Bush is a professor of geosciences at the State University of West Georgia. William J. Neal is a professor of geology at Grand Valley State University. Robert S. Young teaches in the geosciences department at Western Carolina University.

The 2004 hurricane season in Florida devastated an incredible amount of coastline property, demonstrating the dangers of building near the ocean. However, rather than building elsewhere, developers have been rebuilding even bigger houses on the sites of destruction. Although coastline should not be developed at all, it is impossible to convince developers not to build on this appealing land. Therefore, the second best course of action is hazard planning. Coastal communities should be developed with a plan for mitigating and dealing with natural disaster. Architects should also be responsible. If they are unable to convince their clients of the dangers of coastal building, they should at least assess the hazards of a particular building site and design the structure with the dangers in mind. Although politicians often override the regulations that would protect coastal communities from natural disasters, architects can develop sites to reduce the dangers of building on the coast.

David M. Bush, William J. Neal, and Robert S. Young, "After the Storms: Geologists' Perspectives for Architects in Building in Coastal Zones," *Architectural Record,* vol. 192, November 1, 2004, p. 65. Copyright © 2004 by The McGraw-Hill Companies, Inc. All rights reserved. Reproduced by permission.

The stunning 2004 hurricane season highlights the folly of developing high-risk coastal areas. Yet in the wake of the destruction, the emphasis is already being put on rebuilding in the same high-hazard zones. This pattern of coming back "bigger and better" has been repeated numerous times in recent decades—such as the pushes after Hurricane Frederic on the Gulf Coast (1979) and after Hurricane Opal in the Florida Panhandle (1995)—setting the stage for greater financial loss, worsening evacuation efficacy, and increasing the potential for greater loss of life in the next storm.

Simply put, many coastal-zone properties should not be developed. Design and engineering is not going to change the rate of sea-level rise nor lessen the frequency or intensity of storms and their associated winds, waves, storm surge, and runoff. It is true that we have gotten better at predicting storm paths and evacuating threatened areas. We are even designing structures that can withstand much higher winds than in the past. But ultimately, developing high-risk areas is a losing battle, maybe not for the builder, but certainly for the homeowner and the general public.

The rush to the shore in recent decades has resulted in population growth rates three times the national average for areas within 5 miles of the shoreline. The resulting demand for ocean views and beach and waterfront access encourages development in high-to-extreme-risk areas, such as the beachfront, on lowlands adjacent to sounds, and next to finger canals—placing ever-increasing property investments and more residents at risk from the impact of storm winds, waves, and flooding.

The concentration of population and vulnerable development is especially alarming given the projected increase in hurricane frequency and intensity due to changing cyclical climatic patterns and possibly from global warming, which portends an ominous future for coastal disasters. The problem must be addressed now.

Storm History: Learning from the Past

The probability that a hurricane will make landfall at any given point along the coast in any given year is low, and the probability of a great hurricane almost makes such an event seem unlikely; but low probabilities give a false sense of security. If probability is a guidepost, then planners and designers should consider the probability of a major storm occurring during the lifetime of the structure. In that view, storm history tells us that such a storm is almost a certainty. Furthermore, as we've seen from the convergences of Charlie, Ivan, and others, the occurrence of one hurricane does not reduce the likelihood that a similar storm will strike again in the remainder of the season, next year, or in multiple years to come.

Thanks to Weather Service warnings, radio and television communications, and evacuation plans, death tolls from modern hurricanes have declined. But this decline has also led to a false sense of security and contributed to complacency about controlling coastal growth. Hence, while storm deaths have declined, damage totals have increased dramatically. Much of this cost is born not by coastal residents and developers, but by all taxpayers and any member of the general public who pays an insurance premium. Not surprisingly, greater degree of property loss parallels the number of unsafe developments, those where the carrying capacity of the coastal zone has been exceeded.

Population growth has reached such levels that it has begun to exceed the capacity for safe evacuation. Evacuation time in some areas takes considerably longer than the minimum time allowed for advance evacuation warning (as little as 9 to 12 hours).

Our knowledge of coastal hazards, carrying capacity, storm history, and risk mapping has been in place since the 1970s, but the coastal community at large has ignored this available science. Federal and state regulations of the coastal zone under the Coastal Zone Management Act, the Coastal Barrier

Resources Act, the National Flood Insurance Program, and similar programs also have failed to check unsafe development or the escalating costs of storm damage. For example, much of the northern end of North Topsail Beach, North Carolina, is in a coastal barrier resources zone designated so that newly constructed homes and businesses are not eligible for national flood insurance. However, after Hurricane Fran (1996), federal assistance was provided to the town to rebuild infrastructure such as roads and bridges, which allow for future continued development, thus defeating the goal of the federal program.

Hazards, Economics, and Politics

Nature is not the only arena of the coastal zone, and hazardous processes are not the only players. Property owners, planners, and public officials can mitigate the impact of hazards, but their domain is one of politics and economics, governed by a unique set of rules. Our survey of coastal communities reveals great diversity in responses, yet enough similarities exist among communities to make several generalizations.

One incongruity in coastal development is that development sites are chosen on the basis of market forces, not Nature's forces. As a result, most coastal communities came into existence without hazard planning, although there are a few exceptions, such as Kiawah Island, South Carolina, and Seaside, Florida. In older developments, residents learned from experience, and low-risk sites tended to be developed first, leaving high-risk areas, such as the New Jersey Shore and Orange Beach, Alabama, to accommodate today's spiraling growth. With most recent coastal development, the emphasis is on build and sell, not analysis of hazard risk, hazard mitigation, or future relocation. Furthermore, the construction industry prospers in the post-storm rush to rebuild. As a result, one catastrophe often sets the stage for bigger catastrophes. Post-catastrophe "recovery" becomes a time of shock and haste to put things right again. Instead of implementing careful relocation and risk reduction, recovery efforts result in houses and multihousing units rebuilt "bigger and better" in the same high-risk zones.

Recommendations: The Rules of the Sea

Our first recommendation to the thoughtful architect is to assess the hazards of a particular building site with the goal of steering clients out of high-risk areas. If a project must be designed within a potential coastal hazard area, we offer the following guidance: recognizing the physical processes active within coastal environments is the fundamental step toward defining hazard areas, and it forms the basis of a coastal-processes approach to site selection, building design, and property damage mitigation. There are also other important factors to keep in mind.

Our first recommendation to the thoughtful architect is to assess the hazards of a particular building site with the goal of steering clients out of high-risk areas.

First, the coastal zone is unique and requires unique management strategies. Coastal environments are far more dynamic than inland areas. The traditional grid-development pattern and related construction used inland is inappropriate for the coastal zone and increases the probability of impact by natural processes.

Moreover, individual coastal physical processes must be identified and understood from a holistic perspective. Beaches, dunes, marshes, maritime forests, and the offshore are part of one large interrelated geobiologic system. Building in the path of natural processes creates the hazard.

Additionally, building siting, design, and property-damage mitigation must take into account the entire character of coastal processes and environments. Solutions need to be broader than considering single risk factors or individual sites.

Development plans must take into account the regional effects of sea-level rise, erosion rates, flood zones, overwash zones, inlet proximity, and other coastal processes/hazards. Property-damage potential is site-specific, but each site is different. The storm-to-storm crisis approach should be replaced by established long-term solutions for this long-term problem, such as planned relocation.

Building siting, design, and property-damage mitigation must take into account the entire character of coastal processes and environments.

Finally . . . regional and site planning should always seek to maintain the natural environment. Sand volume must be preserved or increased. Vegetation cover provides natural protection. When a landform is altered, its stability is altered. Stabilization may be augmented by adding and anchoring sediment, planting natural species, or even constructing artificial landforms. Alterations due to development should be repaired. Damage to the natural setting reduces the afforded natural protection. Such damage must be repaired to mitigate future property damage. In many cases, such efforts will entail little more than restoring small areas to their pre-development state by rebuilding dunes and planting grasses and other maritime vegetation.

Architects Should Be Responsible

Hazard assessments and mitigation recommendations are the realm of scientists and engineers, but implementation falls into the political/legal arena. While protective regulations such as dune protection ordinances, setback laws, and zoning are based on scientific principles, the rules of politics often override the rules of the sea. One example is the overuse of building variances. In some coastal communities, such variances seem to be the rule rather the exception, again putting property and people at risk. Florida has granted variances for buildings to be constructed seaward of the construction setback line, and in Kill Devil Hills and South Nags Head, North Carolina, where shore hardening structures are not permitted, temporary sandbag walls and groins have been permitted, defeating the purpose of regulation. The architect has the final opportunity to reduce hazard vulnerability in developing site and building plans that follow the rules of the sea.

13

People Should Not Live in Hazard-Prone Areas

Seth R. Reice

Seth R. Reice is an associate professor of biology and ecology at the University of North Carolina, Chapel Hill. Reice researches biodiversity and is an ecological consultant for the restoration of the Rio Tibagi in Parana, Brazil. His published works include The Silver Lining: The Benefits of Natural Disasters.

Disturbances in the ecosystem, even in the form of natural disasters, are essential to maintaining biodiversity. Fires, floods, and hurricanes are a part of the natural cycle and the most appropriate response to these disasters is to avoid living in areas which they are likely to occur. Although people should have the freedom to live where they choose, city and regional planners should be mindful of areas that are most likely to experience natural disasters and regulate or forbid building in these danger zones. For instance, many oceanfront areas have a high likelihood of being destroyed in a hurricane and should not be developed. Building on floodplains should also be illegal. These easily disturbed areas are critical parts of ecosystems. By refusing to build on them, people are not only safeguarding themselves from natural disaster but protecting the environment as well.

Disturbances are essential to maintaining biodiversity, and biodiversity is essential for the healthy functioning of ecosystems and the stability and efficiency of ecosystem services. Once we understand ecosystems and how they work, we need the means to achieve them and to sustain their biodiversity and health. We have learned that disturbances are natural, and fires, floods, and hurricanes are bound to happen as part of natural cycles. Let's get smart. Let's try to get out of their way. Here are a few ideas on how to achieve these goals.

Disturbances and Development

Ecologically based zoning is an excellent place to start on our path to restoring well-functioning ecosystems. Land development must be ecologically sound and controlled to minimize the risk to life and property. Those allowed to build in disturbance-prone zones will lose their buildings in time. Freedom of choice and free exercise of property rights must therefore be tempered by risk aversion and sensitivity to ecological realities. City and regional planners in all areas know what the ecological risks are in their communities and where the risks are greatest. We need to use that information to regulate development in flood, fire, storm, and erosion-prone areas, which often are home to unique species and communities. In protecting our homes and ourselves from natural disturbances, we are also protecting our ecosystems. In building structures, our goal should be long-term ecological compatibility. Below are some zoning guidelines for minimizing losses due to inevitable natural disturbances.

Don't Build on the Beach

Beachfront property is highly desirable. Along the barrier islands and the Outer Banks of North Carolina, Georgia, and Virginia this property is the most expensive. It offers the best view of the beach. Simultaneously, it has the highest likelihood of being destroyed and washed away in a hurricane. A major storm will not only tear the roofs off houses, and the houses off their foundations, but it can and will reclaim the beach itself for the ocean. Whole dunes and the houses built on them are commonly washed away in storms. Wallace Kaufman and Orrin Pilkey, in their excellent book *The Beaches Are Moving,* explain that the natural state of barrier islands is to erode at one end and reform at the other. This is an ongoing process, accelerated during storms. The movement of barrier islands is absolutely normal, and we know the risks. The only way to solve the problem of beach erosion is not to build there in the first place. Let's just say "no" to building on beaches.

Stop Development in Floodplains

Rivers *will* flood, and there is no mystery, no surprise about this. If you build a home or a business in a river's floodplain, it is bound to get flooded and perhaps destroyed. Many communities now have zoning ordinances that rely on estimates of the "100 Year Floodplain," the level that the extreme event— the one flood in one hundred years—will reach. The assumption is that building outside of that zone is safe. Flood frequency is increasing in urbanized areas because the storm waters run off the paved and built-up surfaces. So, what was once the 100-year flood mark is now exceeded far more often. These measures need to be reevaluated. Recall that floodplains and their wetlands are vital ecosystems, providing many ecosystem services to us. When we build there, we compromise the ability of the wetland ecosystem to function.

Insurance companies (and the U.S. government's flood insurance program) need to set their rates according to ecological reality. If the ecological risk is high because the development is in a high-hazard zone, then the owner should be required to pay a very high—even prohibitive—insurance premium based on that risk. Some progress is being made on this issue. After the Great Mississippi Flood of 1993, flood victims were compensated but were not permitted to rebuild in the floodplain. People with flood losses should get reimbursed only if they rebuild in a flood-free zone. Let's just say "no" to building on floodplains. . . .

Living with the Land

We want the world that we leave to our children and grandchildren to be as healthy and beautiful as the world we live in, or even better. We want to raise the standard of living for the poorest members of society. To attain these goals, we must protect and preserve healthy, functioning ecosystems and their biodiversity. These goals must be linked, since to achieve a sustainable future, we must couple healthy ecosystems with healthy, fulfilled people.

Development is sustainable. Growth is not. We need sufficient land to support healthy ecosystems and preserve biodiversity. The size of the preserves must be large enough to support our most wide-ranging species and be linked with extensive natural corridors. This preservation includes maintaining large-enough tracts of natural landscapes so that disturbances can occur without impinging inordinately on human settlements.

People with flood losses should get reimbursed only if they rebuild in a flood-free zone.

As we accept the need for large natural areas, we must also accept natural disturbances as a part of life. We need the rejuvenating and restorative effects of disturbances: to create patchiness in the habitat, to permit the continued existence of biodiversity, and to maintain ecosystem health. Despite our best efforts, we cannot successfully control nature, and we must learn to live with it. We must understand and accept that ecosystems are dynamic, not static. Those fearsome fires, floods, and storms are essential to the maintenance of biodiversity and to the healthy functioning of ecosystems. We must develop our human communities with an understanding and appreciation of the critical role of disturbance in our ecosystems and our own life-support systems. We must reconnect to the ecosystem and live in accord with it. If we use our heads and accept nature's realities we will live eco-logically. Along that path lies a sustainable and ecologically viable future.

14

Relief Agencies Must Dispel Myths About Natural Disasters

Claude de Ville de Goyet

Claude de Ville de Goyet served as the director of the Emergency Preparedness and Disaster Relief Coordination Program of the Pan American Health Organization, regional office for the Americas of the World Health Organization (PAHO/WHO). Until his retirement from this position in April 2002, de Ville de Goyet was a member of a task force established within the International Strategy for Disaster Reduction (ISDR). He is presently a consultant for PAHO/WHO and other organizations.

Many of the myths about the needs and problems of people who have experienced a natural disaster are detrimental and false. For example, the belief that the bodies of the dead cause a major risk of disease leads people to quickly and unceremoniously dispose of corpses, which is a terrible blow to people already suffering from the disaster. In fact, dead bodies do not pose the major health risk that some doctors have wrongly claimed. The myth that victims are helplessly waiting for Western intervention is also not true. Most of the survivors are rescued by local workers. When international workers rush in to disaster-stricken areas, they often do not understand the local conditions and needs and only contribute to the confusion. The myth that sending food, blankets, and other goods is helpful also diminishes the effectiveness of relief aid. Unrequested goods are inappropriate and burdensome. What victims really need is financial support so that they can rebuild their lives. Educating donors so that they know how to best aid disaster victims is the best way to ensure successful relief efforts.

The international response to the tragic earthquake in Turkey [in 1999] highlights the need to reassess the myths and realities surrounding disasters, and to find ways to stop these destructive tales. The myth that dead bodies cause a major risk of disease, as reiterated in all large natural disasters from the earthquake in Managua, Nicaragua (1972) to Hurricane Mitch and now the Turkish earthquake, is just that, a myth. The bodies of victims from earthquakes or other natural disasters do not present a public health risk of cholera, typhoid fever or other plagues mentioned by misinformed medical doctors. In fact, the few occasional carriers of the communicable diseases who were unfortunate victims of the disaster are a far lesser threat to the public than they were while alive. Often overlooked is the unintended social consequence of the precipitous and unceremonious disposal of corpses. It is just one more severe blow to the affected population, depriving them of their human right to honour the dead with a proper identification and burial. The legal and financial consequences of the lack of a death certificate will add to the suffering of the survivors for years to come. Moreover, focussing on the summary disposal, superficial 'disinfection' with lime, mass burial, or cremation of corpses requires important human and material resources that should instead be allocated to those who survived and remain in critical condition.

PAHO's experience in the aftermath of the earthquake in Mexico City showed that health authorities and the media can work together to inform the public, make possible the identification of the deceased and the return of their bodies to the families in a climate free of unfounded fears of epidemics.

No Need for Rescuers

The myth that the affected population is helplessly waiting for the Western world to save it is also false, especially in countries with a large but unevenly distributed medical population. In fact, only a handful of survivors owe their lives to foreign teams. Most survivors owe their lives to neighbours and local authorities. When foreign medical teams arrive, most of the physically accessible injured have already received some medical attention. Western medical teams are not necessarily most appropriate to the local conditions.

Many will have found that press coverage of the Turkey earthquake created a sense of déjà vu: international rescue teams rushing in were made to look as though they were saving victims neglected by incompetent or corrupt local authorities. We have seen the same cliché after major earthquakes and hurricanes in the Americas.

Too much of the assistance is directed to non-issues or myths.

Disaster-stricken countries appreciate external assistance when directed to real problems. Unfortunately, too much of the assistance is directed to non-issues or myths. For example, a common myth is that any kind of international assistance is needed and needed now, while experience shows that a hasty response that is not based on familiarity with local conditions and meant to complement national efforts only contributes to the chaos. It is often better to wait until genuine needs have been assessed. Many also believe that disasters bring out the worst in human behaviour, but the truth is that while isolated cases of antisocial behaviour exist the majority of people respond spontaneously and generously.

The myth that the affected population is too shocked and helpless to take responsibility for its own survival is superseded by the realty that, on the contrary, many find new strength during an emergency—as is evidenced by the thousands of volunteers who spontaneously united to sift through the rubble in search of victims after the 1985 Mexico City earthquake or the one in Turkey. Such cross-cultural dedication to the common good of so many volunteers and institutions, without red tape or petty institutional turf fights, might keep alive our faith in humankind and society.

Returning to Normal Takes Time

The myth that things return to normal within a few weeks is especially pernicious. The truth is that the effects of a disaster last a long time. Disaster-affected countries deplete many of their financial and material resources in the immediate post-impact phase. The bulk of the need for external assistance is in the restoration of normal primary healthcare services, water systems, housing and income-producing work. Social and mental health problems will appear when the acute crisis has subsided and the victims feel (and often are) abandoned to their own means. Successful relief programmes gear their operations to the fact that international interest wanes as needs and shortages become more pressing.

Natural disasters such as the tragic Turkey earthquake do not result in imported diseases that are not already present in the affected area, and they do not provoke secondary disasters through outbreaks of communicable diseases. Proper resumption of public heath services, such as immunisation and sanitation measures, control and disposal of waste, and special attention to water quality and food safety, will ensure the safety of the population and of relief workers.

Send Money, Not Blankets

It is essential that the press and the donor community be aware of what is good practice and malpractice in public health emergency management. Past sudden-impact natural disasters in the Americas and elsewhere have shown the need for international contributions in cash and not in kind. This ensures that allocation of resources is field-driven by evidence of what is needed on site. The population in Turkey does not need used clothing, household or prescription medicines, blood and blood derivatives, medical or paramedical personnel of teams, field hospitals and modular medical units. They want, as do any victims of disaster, to rebuild safer houses, put their children in school and get back to their lives. Unilateral contributions of unrequested goods are inappropriate, burdensome, and divert resources from what is needed most.

There are lessons to be learned. While it is true that the Turkish authorities were unprepared, who is ever ready for a disaster of this magnitude? The World Health Organisation should have done more to strengthen local capacity, but with what resources? The US and other countries spent millions of dollars to dispatch search and rescue teams (who arrived after the most critical first hours or days) to a country where thousands of local medical doctors volunteered their services. A small part of this money could have been more effectively applied in preparedness and prevention activities.

Education Is Key

We need to educate donors just as we need to educate potential victims of disasters. A little preparedness can go a long way toward alleviating the 'secondary' disasters often visited on countries. Increased funding for the US Office of Foreign Disaster Assistance for disaster preparedness and prevention in the 'third world', and more funding from other bilateral or international agencies, could help matters.

If donors would commit now to strengthen the local capacity to respond to future disasters in Turkey, in the disaster-prone countries of the Americas, and other places, and learn what is important and what is futile in helping countries, the world would be better off.

15

Relief Agencies Should Study Past Disasters

Thomas R. DeGregori

Thomas R. DeGregori is a professor of economics at the University of Houston and a member of the Board of Directors of the American Council on Science and Health. He has served overseas as a development economist and adviser to donor organizations and developing countries. His recent publications include Origins of the Organic Agriculture Debate, The Environment, Our Natural Resources and Modern Technology, *and* Bountiful Harvest: Technology, Food Safety, and the Environment.

The world has discovered a lot in the last thirty years about the best ways to institute post-disaster intervention; however, there is still much to examine and learn. Care should be taken that relief aid does not make situations worse. For example, providing goods or food that a country does not need can hurt its economy as the prices of locally produced items drop. Aid agencies have also learned that it is better to collect monetary donations than goods because it is expensive and difficult to transport goods, which often turn out to be unusable. Understanding the most common problems with relief aid and educating the public on the most effective ways to assist in relief efforts is critical to response effectiveness. It is most important, however, for relief agencies and governments to evaluate each relief effort, learning from the experience in order to provide even more successful relief the next time a natural disaster occurs.

Over the last thirty years, we have learned a lot about what to do and not do in post-disaster intervention. There are cases where relief aid may have actually made the situation worse rather than better. Two mid-1970s summer earthquakes in Central America did little damage to the crops in the field. Yet food aid was a major part of the relief effort. The result was that many farmers did not harvest their crops either because the price was too low or because their tool sheds and equipment had been damaged in the earthquake. The following spring, many farmers failed to plant for the same reasons. A post-relief analysis concluded that it would have been more helpful to send down farm equipment and building materials.

The media response to disaster for decades has been a call for food, clothing, and blankets, which were to be collected and sent to the effected region. A decade ago, I had an op-ed in the *Houston Chronicle*, (August 14, 1994) in which I made the case against collecting and attempting to send commodities and argued instead for sending money. Even though I was merely relating what aid agencies had learned over the previous two decades from their mistakes, the idea of simply giving money was still novel and even radical to some and not fully accepted.

In 1994, I asked Houstonians to help alleviate the suffering in Rwanda and Haiti by opening their wallets and not their pantries if they really wanted to do some good. Callous as it sounded to some, the best way to have a positive impact, then and now, was to send money through reputable private voluntary organizations and not send food, clothing, or medicine directly overseas. Ten years on, amidst all this tragedy, I am heartened that the media itself and many of those whom they interviewed made this same argument. It is far easier, once a reputable organization is identified, to go to the Internet and give a donation using your credit card than it is to search through the house for items and then haul them off to a collection center, where they will likely collect dust and do little if any good. Giving money is both easier and more effective.

Because of past mistakes in sending the wrong forms of aid, it is now standard procedure for U.S. ambassadors to give an initial sum of money from a special fund for that purpose while donors like USAID send out a needs assessment team or teams before sending further aid. Each disaster is unique and generates its own special needs—and in the case of the tsunami, different regions suffered differently and need different kinds of help. There are, however, enough underlying commonalities so that a team of experts going out to be briefed by local authorities will know what questions to ask and what to look for on the ground. About five years or so ago, when interviewing AID officials about our disaster response, one of the most respected TV journalists asked pointedly if the whole process was a bit too bureaucratic. In the current crisis, similar questions are being asked, but they are more respectful, giving experts an opportunity to explain the reason for a needs assessment team.

Some Common Problems with Aid Efforts

Transportation problems. Elements of the situation that I described in 1994 resemble the current situation. In 1994, people were starving in Rwanda, as they are today in Darfur and in some of the remote areas of Sumatra. Neither in 1994 nor today can food collected in Houston get to where it is needed. In 1994, airports at Goma, Kigali, and Entebbe were so tight that shipments couldn't get through unless those in charge were assured they carried a top-priority item and that there was some mechanism for distribution to those in need. It is clear in the current crisis that what is holding back aid is not the lack of available commodities but the breakdown in the local transportation infrastructure. Intense coverage of this crisis has highlighted the difficulty of getting aid to those who

101

need it. Local transportation bottlenecks occur more often than the public might realize.

Sending the right type of food. Disaster intervention has become something of a science in the last three decades. For famines, food is carefully formulated to meet nutritional needs in the particular areas involved. Sending culturally-appropriate food is also important, and difficult to do with large volumes of small donations. Who will sift out cans of pork and beans from shipments to Muslim countries? What works well in Houston may not fare as well in other cultures.

Having the right tools on-site. Another practical point that probably goes without saying but is worth a mention here: shipping canned goods to refugees in Third World countries like Rwanda helps no one if people don't have can openers and can't read the directions on the cans. In most if not all of the impacted areas of the tsunami, people probably had can openers that are now lost in the rubble.

Getting usable medicine to victims. Similarly, in 1994, there was a group in Houston trying to collect medicine for Rwanda refugees—but there was no way that the medicine would reach its target as no reputable physician would use medicine of unknown provenance. Getting medicine abroad is another matter best left to the experts. Many critical vaccines and antibiotics so desperately needed in disaster areas are also temperature-sensitive. One of the biggest challenges for relief providers is to maintain what's called the "cold chain" all the way to the field.

Correctly identifying disease. In the early 1990s, word somehow got to the donors that there was an outbreak of meningitis in a disaster area. Only after medicine was sent out was it learned that it was actually cholera. That two diseases so vastly different in so many obvious ways could be confused shows the breakdown in communication that can be created by the chaos of a disaster.

Needs shift quickly. In Rwanda, cholera was the original problem, but suddenly the major medical concern became shigella. Relief workers had to wait for medicine to combat shigella, which quickly became the top-priority cargo at crowded airports.

Clothing supplies can spread disease. Most countries are fearful of spreading disease, so shipments of relief clothes and blankets aren't allowed unless they are properly cleaned and fumigated. This is most easily done in gigantic blocks, which are containerized and then shipped in bulk by those who do it regularly.

Sometime in the late 1980s or early 1990s, well-meaning groups in Houston collected goods for earthquake victims in Central America. Six months later, we saw and read news stories on how most of the donated items were still collecting dust in warehouses. If the food and clothing were not worth shipping from Houston to Central America by truck, they will most certainly not be worth flying to Asia or Africa from most anywhere in the United States.

The Best Way to Give Relief

Some of the things we've learned from past efforts:

1. Release funds to local authorities and quickly dispatch needs assessment teams in order to prioritize the delivery of aid. Obviously, the more rapid the response, the better and more effective it is, as long as it is the right response. Better a brief interval to get things right then to clog the system with the wrong deliveries.

2. Those who wish to help should give money and give it as quickly as possible. Many relief NGOs (nongovernmental organizations) may already have ongoing projects in the area, staffed by locals and others who know the language and can be the best first responders if they have the funds to get what they need.

3. Give commodities only if requested by those on the scene who know the needs and have the mechanisms to have the commodities delivered and used. The one exception to the cash-is-best theory of disaster relief is when there is a call from those on the scene for a specific item such as blood. Such a call implies, or should imply, that there is a mechanism in place to get the blood from where it is to where it is needed. This sort of call is most likely for an in-country disaster. Even if the blood that you give simply ends up in a local blood bank, it frees up other blood to be used immediately.

4. When possible, make purchases of relief items in the disaster area itself. This provides cash inflow that will later help the economy to rebuild. Even in some of the poorest areas, there may be already-existing aid programs with stocks of needed supplies. If it is locally obtained, it is more likely to fit into the culture and be acceptable.

Relief agencies keep warehouses stocked with items most needed in disasters. But, for instance, if they have a feeding program for pregnant women, they would rightly be hesitant to release food stocks in response to a disaster, even though that need may be greater and more immediate, since to do so could put their life-saving programs in jeopardy. These groups must have funding to restock supplies when disasters deplete them.

Fighting Disease

It is a truism in disaster intervention that far more people die from disease outbreaks after the event than directly from the disaster. Children are particularly vulnerable to dehydration and death from diarrhea diseases. In addition to provision of clean water, antibiotics are needed because diarrhea is likely to be endemic to the region already and to spread rapidly before assistance can be rendered. Even after the diarrhea-causing microorganisms are eliminated, it is difficult for already-malnourished children to rebuild the epithelial lining of the gastrointestinal track so that they can take in water.

Thirty years ago, one would see the very sad sight of children attached to IVs in an effort to rehydrate them. One knew that the failure rate was high. In the late 1970s, a cheaper, more effective treatment, Oral Rehydration Therapy (ORT), was discovered, involving the use of common items—sugar, salt, and an electrolyte. Many women in Third World countries already know how to prepare them and have the ingredients on hand. Oral rehydration salts (ORS) packaged with language and pictorial instructions understandable to recipient populations are available in the tsunami disaster region (I have bought them for personal use in several of these places). The technology of ORT may be simple, but sophisticated scientific research discovered it.

Science and technology have also produced antibiotics that are more heat stable, are often in high-tech packaging that help to keep them at the right temperature, and arrive via more reliable means of transportation—all of which makes it more likely the antibiotics will be effective. Thanks to the global effort to expand immunization, the vast majority of children in the tsunami area will have been immunized for six or seven basic diseases in contrast to thirty years ago when this was the case for only a small minority in the region and throughout the Third World.

There is an array of other basic knowledge about disaster intervention for floods, famines, earthquakes, hurricanes/typhoons, and now tsunamis that is almost the exact opposite of what was conventional wisdom three decades ago. And there is new technology that can help. We have all now seen the importance of helicopters in delivering aid, and most of us by now know about the use of sniffer dogs, robotics, and other specialized equipment to rescue people trapped in buildings collapsed by earthquakes.

The globalization of disaster intervention made possible by modern communication and transportation technologies has in recent decades begun to close some of the gap in loss of life from disasters between developed and developing countries. Thus the admonition to buy locally is coupled with a vast array of technologies and capabilities that are rushed to a region from all parts of the globe.

Utilizing Technology

Unfortunately, there are some things that we could do better thirty or so years ago than we can today. Malaria and dengue fever are endemic to many of the areas hardest hit by the tsunami. The flooding water is likely to have cleaned out the mosquito larvae, creating a brief period of reduced disease and an opportunity to reduce it further. But with stagnant pools of water, the area will be quickly re-colonized by mosquitoes. Because of the breakdown of the material structure and to some extent social structure of villages, local defense measures against disease vectors, however inadequate they may have been to start with, will now be non-existent. These diseases will quickly return with a vengeance, as will other diseases, assaulting a physically and psychologically weakened population.

Unfortunately, there are some things that we could do better thirty or so years ago than we can today.

What is needed is the provision of the most effective weapon against the disease vectors, which in the case of the mosquito is DDT. Tragically, that won't happen thanks to activists who got it banned a little over three decades ago by the U.S., followed by European countries and in effect all donor organizations. In addition, water needs to be chlorinated even if it is not being drunk because, having been mixed with sewage, it will be harboring an extraordinary array of diseases.

Again, at least one of the activist groups opposes the use of chlorine, but in this case their opposition is unlikely to be a deterrent to its eventual use.

We need to distinguish between those NGOs that are actually in the field helping people and the activist NGOs that do absolutely nothing to help those in need but somehow claim to be speaking and acting on their behalf. These latter groups are the ones that preferred to see Africans starve during a famine rather than have them eat perfectly good donated transgenic grain. They claimed that there was enough non-transgenic food available in Southern Africa to feed the famine-stricken populations, but none of them used any of their $100 million+ annual budgets to buy any of the allegedly available food for distribution to the needy. NGOs routinely oppose all dam construction, construction that could provide water for irrigation and/or electricity. They oppose the economic development that protects people while blaming technology for all the ills of the world, including the tsunami. Yet they live in developed countries and enjoy the benefits of the technologies that they oppose.

Clearly, one of the biggest problems that we face is not the destructive force of nature but the organized ideological opposition to the effective use of modern technology. One of the most important things we can do after donating money is to try to put pressure on donor groups, including our own government, to make use of the most effective means of saving lives of children and adults from malaria, dengue fever, and other mosquito borne diseases: *use DDT.*

In my work as a development economist, I have seen far more poverty and human tragedy than I really cared to see. I have been troubled over the last two decades as I watched decent, caring people generously responding to the misfortune of others in ways that were ineffective and in some ways counter-productive, whether through misguided aid efforts or through opposition to the scientific and economic developments that enable populations to help themselves. Fortunately, there now seems to be better understanding in the media and in the public about how to respond to a disaster. Like all human inquiry, it is a continuous learning process and a battle against those who would have us reverse course. It is the scientific method applied to life's problems: learn from one's experience in order to do better the next time.

16

Hurricane Katrina Revealed the Weakness of U.S. Emergency Response

Paul Light

Paul Light is a professor at New York University's Robert F. Wagner School of Public Service. He writes extensively about federal government reform and organization, the civil service, entitlement programs, and Social Security. He has written many books, including The President's Agenda, *the award-winning* Artful Work: The Politics of Social Security Reform, Pathways to Nonprofit Excellence, *and* Government's Greatest Achievements.

Americans usually choose to ignore the possibility of disaster in their own homes. When Hurricane Katrina hit the Gulf Coast in September 2005, the nation was extremely unprepared for a disaster of that magnitude. Many residents of the disaster zone ignored the evacuation warnings that were issued for two days before the hurricane struck, and relief agencies did not begin to send emergency supplies until after the disaster had left thousands homeless. The chaos that ensued showed that the United States must develop a much better organized and well-funded national preparedness and response system in order to deal more effectively with disasters in the future. Creating such a system

Paul Light, "Preparation, Relief Fall Short: Katrina Should Be Motivation to Act Quickly," *The Atlanta Journal-Constitution,* September 2, 2005. Copyright © by *The Atlanta Journal-Constitution.* Reproduced by permission of the author.

will require time, money, and continued preparation, but it is the best way to prepare for disasters like Hurricane Katrina.

Even as the Gulf Coast states battle to recover from Hurricane Katrina, Washington should take heed of the chaos surrounding the early relief effort. If this is what happens when the nation has two days of warning, imagine the aftermath of a surprise attack using a chemical, biological or nuclear device.

There will be plenty of stories of heroism in coming months as thousands of volunteers descend on the disaster zone. But the hubris is already showing. Thousands of residents ignored the evacuation warnings; many relief agencies waited until the hurricane had passed to start sending supplies and volunteers to jumping-off points in surrounding states; and the president was heading to California as the hurricane moved in.

Although the Department of Homeland Security [DHS] and its Federal Emergency Management Agency are moving at near-light speed to coordinate an unprecedented relief effort built around DHS' National Response Plan, the nation must get even faster in the future.

Ironically, a Category 5 hurricane was already on the DHS list of 15 planning scenarios for emergency response. In an effort to give organizations more specific guidance about how to plan for catastrophic events, the department issued the scenarios last winter in the hopes that governments, businesses and charitable organizations would start rehearsing their response.

National Preparedness Is Critical

Unfortunately, a yet-to-be-released survey by New York University suggests that most Americans expect disaster to hit just about anywhere but home. Most have enough canned goods and bottled water in the closet to last a few days, but they want their local police and fire agencies, the Red Cross and charities to tell them what to do in the event of a catastrophe.

The problem with Katrina is that many residents did not listen before the hurricane, and communications were cut off after. Plenty of emergency planners had nightmares about a Category 5 hurricane hitting somewhere, but few woke up and started preparing.

Katrina underscores the urgent need to build a robust national preparedness and response system that can bend and flex to the unique circumstances of natural or human-caused catastrophes. Based on my analysis of hundreds of high-performing organizations identified by the nonpartisan Rand Corp., such a system must be alert to impending catastrophe, agile in implementing well-designed plans for response and recovery, adaptive to surprise events such as the collapse of the New Orleans levees, and aligned so that everyone can pull together, from Washington on down to the initial first responder who shows up at the site of a disaster.

Important Aspects of Disaster Response

Here are the four pillars of a robust response system:

- Alertness to what lies ahead. As Katrina surely suggests, the nation faces many possible catastrophes, some that can be predicted, others unexpected but inevitable. A high-performing response system is constantly scanning a wide range of scenarios while establishing signposts that will trigger the kind of action that would have saved precious time after Katrina had moved on. Katrina gave fair warning, but no terrorist will.

- Agility in recruiting, training, retaining and redeploying a talented, flexible work force. Too many local governments have yet to complete even the most basic training on how to respond to a small-scale catastrophe such as a terrorist bombing at a local shopping center, let alone an attack on a chemical refinery. Even when governments, businesses and charitable organizations think ahead, they rarely do so together, creating a sum less when catastrophe strikes.than the parts

---

Katrina underscores the urgent need to build a robust national preparedness and response system.

Agility also involves making sure first responders can talk to each other on equipment that can survive a major catastrophe.

It is one thing to have a plan in place, quite another to execute it. Doing so requires an agile network of signals that can tell first responders where to go and what to do, especially after the cell towers blow over.

- Adaptability. Although no one can be prepared for every eventuality, a robust system provides enough flexibility in dollars, equipment and 3,000-pound sandbags to bring innovation to bear on unexpected events such as flooding and massive fatalities. Unfortunately, Congress, the president and many governments have been doing homeland security on the cheap or through pork-barrel spending.

- Alignment of all organizations to a central plan. As New Orleans Mayor Ray Nagin complained the day after his levees collapsed, there are "way too many . . . cooks in the kitchen." Having an aligned system means just one cook in the kitchen and hundreds of servers on the front lines. If aligning a system means that governments, businesses and charitable organizations have to cede authority to a single director, so be it. Catastrophe is no time for protecting bureaucratic turf.

Creating a Better Response System

Creating this kind of robust response system requires time, money, constant rehearsal and concentration. And it requires individual organizations that are robust, too. This is why

Homeland Security Secretary Michael Chertoff's recently proposed reorganization is so important to implement. By eliminating needless layers of management and focusing on the most likely scenarios, Chertoff is taking an essential step toward creating a more robust department, which in turn will help create a more robust response system.

If Congress really wants to prepare for future disasters like Katrina, it will attach Chertoff's reforms to whatever relief legislation it is sure to pass in coming weeks. At least in planning for catastrophe, preparedness starts at the top, not the bottom, with clear signals about where to invest, whom to engage and how to coordinate.

17

A Belief in God Can Protect Against Disasters

John Ross Schroeder

John Ross Schroeder is a senior writer for the Good News *magazine.*

The December 2004 tsunami left many people questioning how God could let such a terrible thing happen. However, God was not responsible for the immenseness of the tragedy. That fault lies with people. The destruction of the two natural water breaks, mangroves, and coral reefs by humans allowed the waves to do more damage. The lack of preparation and ignorance of people also intensified the effects of the disaster. According to the prophecies of the Bible, the increasing natural disasters that have been occurring, including the 2004 tsunami, are the signs of the second coming of Christ. The world may be in its last days before judgment day, when believers will experience eternal glory and the unrepentant will be destroyed. Although human beings may use technology and warning systems to protect themselves from natural disasters, the only true protection is to repent and surrender to God.

For several weeks after the disaster, newspapers and magazines regularly devoted several pages to the ongoing effects of the deadly tsunami that struck Dec. 26 [2004]. Poignant accounts of tragic personal losses of family and friends put a human face on mounting death-toll statistics. Encouraging stories of incredible heroism and a groundswell of sympathy, expressed in generous contributions from countries all over the world, reminded us that we are our brother's keeper.

Inevitably many religious leaders reacted with a desire to give both their followers and the general public a philosophical framework in which to deal with these unacceptable events. Some responses might be rather surprising.

The title of one article was "If This Was an Act of God—What Was God Thinking?"

The archbishop of Canterbury, in an article in the Jan. 2 [2005] *Sunday Telegraph,* wrote: "The question—'How can you believe in a God who permits suffering on this scale?' is therefore very much around at the moment, and it would be surprising if it weren't—indeed, it would be wrong if it weren't. The traditional answers will get us only so far." . . .

Not God's Fault

While this was a natural disaster, human culpability in the high casualty toll is greater than most had originally imagined. As one commentator cannily observed, "The Almighty might have His critics over the tsunami, but the actions of humankind made it worse."

That particular writer, environment editor Geoffrey Lean, went on to explain: "In the past, the shores of the Indian Ocean have been protected from tsunamis, tidal waves and the angry seas stirred up by cyclones and typhoons by a double barrier of coral reefs and mangrove swamps. The solid barriers of the reefs broke up and slowed down the waves while the tangled roots and dense vegetation of the mangroves absorbed much of their remaining energy.

"*Yet both have been increasingly destroyed* [by man] *over the past 50 years, leaving coasts, and their people, defenceless*" (*The Independent on Sunday*, Jan. 9, emphasis added throughout).

According to Mr. Lean, only about a third of the world's coral reefs are still healthy, with up to one fifth already destroyed. Fishing (using dynamite), pollution, quarrying for construction materials and global warming (a disputed point) have been named as the primary culprits. Mangroves have also been cut down and removed in favor of tourist resorts and shrimp farming.

Specific areas still protected by healthy coral reefs and mangroves sustained much less damage to property and much less loss of human life. The islands of Diego Garcia and the Maldives, isolated and vulnerable in the Indian Ocean but ringed by coral reefs, serve as two examples.

A Feeble Warning System

The British *Sunday Times* stated: "Scientists feared such a catastrophe was looming. So why were there no warnings?" (Jan. 2). A *USA Today* editorial said: "On the day a tsunami killed 140,000 people, scientists and government officials scattered across the Pacific and Asia had inklings of an impending disaster in time to save lives. Yet even in this age of instant global communications, *the message never reached those in peril*" (Jan. 7).

Bureaucratic bungling was partially to blame. Also the Indian Ocean area has no sophisticated warning system like the one wealthier countries encircling the Pacific Ocean have created for their protection. Holiday time was yet another factor.

American geophysicist Dr. Stuart Weinstein was in his Hawaiian office when the instruments in the Pacific Tsunami Warning Center revealed the massive Indian Ocean quake. Dr. Weinstein's duties embrace 26 nations around the Pacific Rim.

But there was no contact book, plan or emergency telephone links for spreading the alarm for the Indian Ocean area of Southeast Asia.

Nonetheless, everyone available began telephoning what numbers they could muster in the endangered areas. But it was Christmas Day in Hawaii and the day after in Southeast Asia. A lot of people were away from their desks. Telephones rang and rang with no answer. A very few who finally did come to the phone listened a little while and then hung up. Somehow the message didn't get through to them. Finally, Dr. Weinstein broke down and cried because he knew what would inevitably happen.

The Ignorance Factor

Nonetheless, many lives still could have been saved even in the last minutes before the tsunami struck had people known what to do. When people saw the tide suddenly retreating back into the ocean area, a few knew to run the other way to as high a ground as possible. Some heeded their shouts of warning and followed. Many, however, stood around to watch the curious sight only to be engulfed by a fast-moving wall of water minutes later.

We should learn crucial lessons from this! *Ignorance of warning factors spared no one.* Similarly, ignorance of Bible prophecy will undoubtedly prove disastrous in the coming biblical day of visitation.

The Bible is a book full of prophetic warnings. They apply to us individually and directly if we persist in failing to acknowledge that God created a moral universe and fail to govern our actions accordingly.

His Word tells us that in ancient times mankind had become exceedingly wicked in both thought and action (Genesis 6:5). To preserve a tiny remnant of humankind and to protect His plan and purpose for humanity, God destroyed all except

Noah and his family in a greet flood. But first, there were 120 years of merciful warning.

The New Testament calls Noah "a preacher of righteousness" (2 Peter 2:5). But instead of acting on Noah's words of warning, his generation likely only made fun of a preacher who would build a giant boat on dry land—that is, until it began raining for days and days and wouldn't stop. Some of these people no doubt finally believed God and His prophet, but it was far too late.

Ignorance of Bible prophecy will undoubtedly prove disastrous.

We know from Scripture exactly how much time they had from when God decided to act. Had they really repented while there was still time, the Flood wouldn't have happened. The inhabitants of ancient Nineveh repented at Jonah's preaching and they were spared. God is no respecter of persons.

Scripture says that "God waited patiently in the days of Noah while the ark was being built" (1 Peter 3:20, New International Version). The Bible doesn't say whether Noah told his contemporaries exactly how much time they had remaining. But he must have told them in general terms that their days were numbered. Today we ourselves don't know how many months or years remain on the clock—how much time we still have to get our act together.

Peter Warns Our Generation

In principle the warnings of Noah apply today in our modern age. The apostle Peter wrote: "First of all, you must understand that *in the last days* scoffers will come, scoffing and following their own evil desires. They will say, 'Where is this "coming" [of Christ] he promised? Ever since our fathers died, everything goes on as it has since the beginning of creation'" (2 Peter 3:3–4, NIV).

Cynics are usually sinners as well. Jesus Christ Himself said behavior just before the time of His second coming would parallel human conduct in the days of Noah.

At least in principle, God warns the modern descendants of ancient Israel in Leviticus 26 and Deuteronomy 28 of what will happen if they go astray from Him and His laws. The overall message is one of cause and effect. . . .

Jesus Christ delivered His longest prophecy to His disciples not long before His crucifixion and subsequent resurrection. Recorded in Matthew 24, Mark 13 and Luke 21, He spoke of key trends and events that would precede, His return to earth—one of which was "nations . . . *in anguish and perplexity at the roaring and tossing of the sea*" (Luke 21:25, NIV).

Then, near the end of the first century, the apostle John wrote the book of Revelation, outlining world events during the time of the end. This long prophecy, too, foretells that natural disasters will play a major role in human affairs in the end time.

Intensified Natural Disasters

According to information reported by BBC News online, global disasters in general are on the increase. Late last year [2004] the International Strategy for Disaster Reduction (ISDR) released its statistical survey in association with the Centre for Research on the Epidemiology of Disasters at the University of Louvain in Belgium.

Natural disasters will play a major role in human affairs in the end time.

The BBC stated: "Events including earthquakes and volcanoes, floods and droughts, storms, fires and landslides killed about 83,000 people in 2003, up from about 53,000 deaths 13 years earlier, the ISDR said." The BBC report also said that

"254 million people were affected by natural hazards last year—nearly three times as many as in 1990" (Sept. 17, 2004).

The ISDR observed: "Not only is the world globally facing more potential disasters but increasing numbers of people are becoming vulnerable to hazards" (ibid.). An earlier BBC News online report warned that "giant tsunamis, super volcanoes and earthquakes could pose a greater threat than terrorism" (Aug. 9, 2004).

Please note that the disturbing results of these surveys and the resultant observations were all released *before* the giant quake and tsunami that rocked nations surrounding the Indian Ocean a few months later.

Summing Up the Scene

Journalists are not statisticians or experts in monitoring natural disasters. They can only report what scientists and geophysicists tell them. Often the writer's role is one of summing up, tying things together or putting events in context. Columnist Sharon Wright did exactly this for Britain's *Daily Express*:

> "Flooding chaos could become a way of life for all of us— because the impact of the merciless weather *has to be seen in the context of extreme natural phenomena across the world.* One by one over the past 12 months, events have been falling into place like the pieces of a deeply disturbing jigsaw puzzle.

> "Rivers across Britain are bursting their banks. There's no snow [yet] in the Alps.... Bears near St. Petersburg are refusing to hibernate. Rain in the Sahara sent a plague of locusts to Africa.... The list is long and very soon may become endless" (Jan. 14 [2005]).

In addition, a record *eight* hurricanes lashed Atlantic islands and coastal regions in 2004 and the Canadian arctic became so warm last summer [2004] that Eskimos reported seeing wasps there for the first time ever. Extremes in weather may be becoming the norm.

The Book of Revelation's Warnings

The final book of the Bible speaks of major end-time happenings when natural disasters occur in extremes. The time of the end is not a normal time. Revelation talks of gargantuan events with massive numbers of people perishing as a prelude to the second coming of Jesus Christ. We may be on the verge of entering these troubling and tragic times. . . .

Scientists and politicians speak of improved warning systems to lessen the loss of life when disasters do occur. One can applaud any workable protective measures that human beings can implement for themselves. Ultimately, however, our only sure protection is in the Eternal God.

Organizations to Contact

American Red Cross
American Red Cross National Headquarters,
  Washington, DC 20006
(202) 303-4498
e-mail: info@redcross.org
Web site: www.redcross.org

The American Red Cross is a humanitarian organization led by volunteers. In 1905 Congress chartered the American Red Cross to "carry out a system of national and international relief in time of peace, and apply that system in mitigating the suffering caused by pestilence, famine, fire, floods and other great national calamities, and to devise and carry out measures for preventing those calamities." It has chapters all over the United States that aid in local and international disaster mitigation and relief. The American Red Cross publishes a variety of disaster preparedness publications, including *Hurricanes . . . Unleashing Nature's Fury! Winter Storms . . . The Deceptive Killers,* and *Are You Ready for an Earthquake?*

Federal Emergency Management Agency (FEMA)
500 C St. SW, Washington, DC   20472
(800) 621-FEMA
Web site: www.fema.gov

FEMA's mission is to lead the effort to prepare the nation for all hazards and effectively manage federal response and recovery efforts following any national emergencies in the United States. FEMA also initiates proactive mitigation activities, trains first responders, and manages the National Flood Insurance Program and the U.S. Fire Administration. Often FEMA works in partnership with other organizations that are part of the nation's emergency management system. These partners include state and local emergency management agencies, twenty-seven federal agencies, and the American Red Cross. FEMA produces many publications, including the *Report on*

Costs and Benefits of Natural Hazard Mitigation and *Surviving the Storm for Floods*. All of these publications are available on the FEMA Web site.

GeoHazards International (GHI)

200 Town & Country Village, Palo Alto, CA 94301
(650) 614-9050
e-mail: info@geohaz.org
Web site: www.geohaz.org

GeoHazards International has a mission of reducing death and suffering, particularly of children, in the event of natural disasters. The organization focuses on advocacy, preparedness, prevention, and mitigation efforts. GHI is currently managing earthquake safety initiatives in India, Kazakhstan, Tajikistan, and Uzbekistan. These three-year initiatives assess risk, raise awareness, improve school safety, and strengthen the ability of governments and nongovernmental organizations (NGOs) to manage their risk. GHI is also collaborating with the Organization for Economic Cooperation and Development (OECD) in an international effort to improve earthquake safety in schools in at-risk countries. Publications by GHI include the books *Seismic Hazard & Building Vulnerability, Issues in Urban Earthquake Risk,* and *Uses of Earthquake Damage Scenario.*

Oxfam

Oxfam Supporter Relations Oxfam House,
  John Smith Dr., Cowley,
  Oxford OX4 2JY UK
0870-333-2700
Web site: www.oxfam.org.uk

Oxfam is a development, relief, and advocacy organization based in England that works to find lasting solutions to poverty and suffering around the world. The organization was started in 1942 during the Second World War. When the war ended, Oxfam continued its mission of aiding those affected by war and other disasters. Oxfam publishes many print reports, including *The Asian Tsunami: The Challenge After the Jakarta Summit, The Tsunami's Impact on Women,* and *Dealing with Disaster.*

ProVention Consortium

PO Box 372, 17 chemin des Crêts   CH-1211 Geneva 19
  Switzerland
e-mail: provention@ifrc.org
Web site: www.proventionconsortium.org

The ProVention Consortium is a global coalition of governments, international organizations, academic institutions, and private sector and civil society organizations dedicated to increasing the safety of vulnerable communities and to reducing the impact of disasters in developing countries. ProVention is involved in research studies, pilot projects, education and training activities, advocacy initiatives, and policy development. The organization offers many publications, including *Understanding the Economic and Financial Impacts of Natural Disasters, Disaster Risk Reduction: Mitigation and Preparedness in Development and Emergency Programming,* and *Building Safer Cities—the Future of Disaster Risk.*

Public Entity Risk Institute (PERI)

11350 Random Hills Rd., #210, Fairfax, VA 22030
(703) 352-1846 • fax: (703) 352-6339
Web site: www.riskinstitute.org

The Public Entity Risk Institute's mission is to help public, private, and nonprofit organizations with risk management. PERI focuses on the development and delivery of education and training on all aspects of risk management. The institute also serves as a resource center and clearinghouse for all areas of risk management. PERI funds grants and research programs in risk management, environmental impairment liability, and disaster management. PERI's publications include *Characteristics of Effective Emergency Management Structures* and *Dealing with Disaster.*

UNICEF
333 East Thirty-eighth St. (Mail Code: GC-6),
  New York, NY   10016
(212) 686-5522
e-mail: information@unicefusa.org
Web site: www.unicefusa.org

UNICEF became a permanent part of the United Nations in 1953. UNICEF seeks to protect the rights and welfare of children. UNICEF works with other organizations to overcome the obstacles that poverty, violence, disease, and discrimination place in a child's path. UNICEF also works to assist children around the world in the event of a natural disaster. UNICEF publishes the quarterly newsletter *Every Child* as well as an annual report that describes its projects.

U.S. Geological Survey (USGS)
345 Middlefield Rd., Menlo Park, CA   94025
(888) 275-8747
Web site: www.usgs.gov

U.S. Geological Survey collects, monitors, analyzes, and provides scientific information about natural resource conditions, issues, and problems. The USGS seeks to minimize the loss of life and property from natural disasters as well as manage water, biological, energy, and mineral resources. The organization's ten thousand scientists, technicians, and support staff work in more than four hundred locations throughout the United States. USGS publishes many papers that are available on its Web site including *Geography for a Changing World* and *Coastal Vulnerability Assessment of Channel Islands National Park (CHIS) to Sea-Level Rise.*

World Bank
1818 H St. NW, Washington, DC   20433
(202) 473-1000
Web site: www.worldbank.org

The World Bank helps governments in developing countries reduce poverty by providing them with the money and technical expertise they need for a wide range of projects such as building schools, roads, or water wells. The World Bank often provides support in the event of natural disasters. The organization's many reports are available on its Web site. The World Bank also produces many publications available for purchase, such as *Getting to Know the World Bank* and *The Market for Aid.*

World Health Organization (WHO)
Avenue Appia 20   1211 Geneva 27
  Switzerland
+ 41-22-791-21-11
e-mail: info@who.int
Web site: www.who.int

The World Health Organization, established in 1948, is the UN specialized agency for health. WHO's objective, as set out in its constitution, is to help all people attain the highest possible level of health. WHO is heavily involved in health care and disease prevention in the event of natural disasters. Readers can find out more about WHO's projects through its publications, such as the *Bulletin of the World Health Organization,* the *Pan American Journal of Public Health,* and the *World Health Report.*

World Meteorological Association (WMO)
7bis, Avenue de la Paix, Case postale No. 2300
  CH-1211 Geneva 2 Switzerland
+ 41-22-730-81-11
e-mail: wmo@wmo.int
Web site: www.wmo.int

The World Meteorological Organization (WMO) is an intergovernmental organization with a membership of 187 countries and territories. Established in 1950, WMO is an agency of the United Nations that carries out research and provides services focused on meteorology, operational hydrology, and related geophysical sciences. The WMO also seeks to predict natural disasters so that the advance warnings that save lives and property can be issued. WMO's many publications include the *WMO Bulletin* and *World Climate News.*

Bibliography

Books

Patrick L. Abbot — *Natural Disasters.* Boston: McGraw Hill, 2002.

David Alexander — *Confronting Catastrophe: New Perspectives on Natural Disasters.* New York: Oxford University Press, 2000.

Greg Bankoff — *Cultures of Disaster: Society and Natural Hazards in the Philippines.* London: RoutledgeCurzon, 2003.

Charlotte Benson — *Understanding the Economic and Financial Impacts of Natural Disasters.* Washington, DC: World Bank, 2004.

Steven Biel — *American Disasters.* New York: New York University Press, 2001.

Kevin M. Cahill — *Emergency Relief Operations.* New York: Fordham University Press, 2003.

Lorenzo Cotula and Margaret Vidar — *The Right to Adequate Food in Emergencies.* Rome, NY: Food and Agriculture Organization of the United Nations, 2003.

Susan Cutter, ed. — *American Hazardscapes: The Regionalization of Hazards and Disasters.* Washington, DC: Joseph Henry, 2001.

Lee Davis — *Natural Disasters.* New York: Checkmark, 2002.

Richard Gist and Bernard Lubin — *Response to Disaster: Psychosocial, Community, and Ecological Approaches.* Philadelphia: Brunner/Mazel, 1999.

Patricia Grossi and Howard Kunreuther — *Catastrophe Modeling: A New Approach to Managing Risk.* New York: Springer Science+Business Media, 2005.

Aseem Inam — *Planning for the Unplanned: Recovering from Crises in Megacities.* New York: Routledge, 2005.

Timothy M. Kusky — *Geographical Hazards: A Sourcebook.* Westport, CT: Greenwood, 2003.

Bill McGuire — *A Guide to the End of the World.* New York: Oxford University Press, 2002.

Bill McGuire, Ian Mason, and Christopher Kilburn — *Natural Hazards and Environmental Change.* London: Arnold, 2002.

Susan Moeller — *Compassion Fatigue: How the Media Sells Disease, Famine, War, and Death.* New York: Routledge, 1999.

Organisation for Economic Co-operation and Development — *Large-Scale Disasters: Lessons Learned.* Paris: Organisation for Economic Co-operation and Development, 2004.

Mark Pellig — *The Vulnerability of Cities: Natural Disasters and Social Resilience.* London: Earthscan, 2003.

Claire Pirotte, Bernard Husson, and Francois Grunewald   *Responding to Emergencies and Fostering Development: The Dilemmas of Humanitarian Aid.* London: Zed, 1999.

Ben Wisner et al.   *At Risk: Natural Hazards, People's Vulnerability and Disasters.* New York: Routledge, 2004.

Periodicals

Joel Achenbach   "Asian Disaster Gives Insulated America a Chance to Lend a Helping Hand," *Washington Post,* December 30, 2004.

Allison Adato et al.   "Surviving Hell & High Water: Braving Disease, Despair, and the Loss of Everything They Knew, Katrina's Victims Tell Amazing Tales of Tragedy and Heroism," *People Weekly,* September 19, 2005.

The African News Service   "Focus on Disaster Mitigation," October 9, 2002.

The African News Service   "United Nations: Generosity Should Extend to All of the World's Victims," January 12, 2005.

Jonathan Alter   "How to Save the Big Easy," *Newsweek,* September 12, 2005.

Norman P. Aquino   "Weekender: The Day After 14 Years," *BusinessWorld,* July 16, 2004.

Asian Development Bank   "An Initial Assessment of the Impact of the Earthquake and Tsunami of

December 26, 2004 on South and Southeast Asia," 2005.

P.G. Bakir
"Proposal for a National Mitigation Strategy Against Earthquakes in Turkey," *Natural Hazards,* November 2004.

Michael Behar
"When Earth Attacks! Tsunamis, Volcanoes, Hurricanes, Landslides—the Single Certain Thing About Nature's Killers Is That They Will Strike Again and Again. Our Only Defense: Even Better Prediction and Protection," *Popular Science,* May 1, 2005.

Gloria Borger
"Coming Up Short: President Bush's Response to Damage Wrought by Hurricane Katrina," *U.S. News & World Report,* September 12, 2005.

John Carey
"Let That Be a Warning; What Katrina Can Teach About Handling Natural Disasters and Energy Better," *Business Week,* September 12, 2005.

Sarah Childress
"Critical Condition; The Health Crisis: Contaminated Water. Dysfunctional Hospitals. The City's Medical Challenge Is Just Beginning," *Newsweek,* September 12, 2005.

John Cloud
"Mopping New Orleans: What Will It Take to Disinfect the City? On the Ground with the Army Corps of Engineers as It Cleans Up Katrina's Deadly Muck," *Time,* September 19, 2005.

Andrew Coyne — "The Economics of Compassion," *National Post,* January 5, 2005.

Martin R. Degg and David K. Chester — "Seismic and Volcanic Hazards in Peru: Changing Attitudes to Disaster Mitigation," *Geographical Journal,* June 2005.

Lori Dengler — "The Role of Education in the National Tsunami Hazard Mitigation Program," *Natural Hazards,* May 2005.

The Economist — "Asia's Devastation," December 29, 2004.

Richard K. Eisner — "Planning for Tsunami: Reducing Future Losses Through Mitigation," *Natural Hazards,* May 2005.

David P. Fidler — "The Indian Ocean Tsunami and International Law," *ASIL Insight,* January 2005.

Financial Express — "Make Disaster Mitigation a Part of the Relief and Rehabilitation Package," January 10, 2005.

Tracy Ford — "Communications Needs," *RCR Wireless,* September 5, 2005.

Alice Fothergill and Lori A. Peek — "Poverty and Disasters in the United States: A Review of Recent Sociological Findings," *Natural Hazards,* May 2004.

Nancy Gibbs — "The Aftermath," *Time,* September 12, 2005.

Peter S. Goodman   "Aid Arrives, but Often Not in Equal Amounts," *Washington Post,* January 9, 2005.

Jeff Greenwald   "Everyone Here Has Post-Traumatic Stress," *Salon,* January 20, 2005.

Jill Iliffe   "Collective Responses Achieve Better Outcomes," *Australian Nursing Journal,* February 2005.

Matthew E. Kahn   "The Death Toll from Natural Disasters: The Role of Income, Geography, and Institutions," *Review of Economics and Statistics,* May 2005.

Suvendrini Kakuchi   "Tsunami Impact: Community Education Urged to Divert Disasters," *IPS–Inter Press Service,* January 19, 2005.

Patrick J. Kiger   "Dealing with Disaster: Part 1 of 2," *Workforce Management,* November 1, 2004.

Jason Kingsley   "Early Warning Systems: Practical Before Convenient and the Local Opinion," *Early Warning Systems: Interdisciplinary Observation and Policies from a Local Government Perspective,* 2005.

Yasuko Kuwata and Shiro Takada   "Effective Emergency Transportation for Saving Human Lives," *Natural Hazards,* September 2004.

Kathryn   "Tsunami Relief, Rehabilitation Aid
McConnell   Simultaneous, Natsios Says," *African
                   News Service,* January 28, 2005.

Donald G.   "How Nature Changes History," *New
McNeil Jr.   York Times,* January 2, 2005.

D. Murali   "Let Not Financing Be a Disaster
                   After Rapid Onset of Natural Disas-
                   ters," *Business Line,* January 6, 2005.

Anna Murline,   "To the Rescue," *U.S. News & World
Angie C. Marek,   Report,* September 12, 2005.
and Silla Brush

Jakob Oetama   "Part 1 of 2: Powering the Media
                   Dynamics for Common Good,"
                   Jakarta Post, March 21, 2005.

Maria Perez-Lugo   "The Mass Media and Disaster
                   Awareness in Puerto Rico: A Case
                   Study of the Floods in Barrio Tor-
                   tugo," *Organization & Environment,*
                   March 2001.

Douglas Quan   "Aid Effort Draws Critics," *Press En-
                   terprise,* January 25, 2005.

Mustafa Adbur   "Environment: Disaster and Health,"
Rahim   *Dhaka Courier,* April 8, 2005.

Amanda Ripley   "How Did This Happen? The Hurri-
                   cane Was the Least of Our Surprises.
                   Why a Natural Disaster Became a
                   Man-Made Debacle—and What This

Catastrophe Says About Our Rescue Capabilities Four Years After 9/11," *Time*, September 12, 2005.

Grace Rollins "It Shouldn't Have to Take an Earthquake," *Yale Herald*, February 2, 2001.

Sally Satel "The Therapy Reflex," *National Review*, January 14, 2005.

State News Service "Tsunami Relief Done Well Becomes Future Model, Clinton Says," April 26, 2005.

Eva Thomas "The Lost City; What Went Wrong; Devastating a Swath of the South, Katrina Plunged New Orleans into Agony. The Story of a Storm—and a Disastrously Slow Rescue," *Newsweek*, September 12, 2005.

Joyti Thottam "How Much Will Really Go to the Victims?" *Time*, January 17, 2005.

Pamela von Gruber "Emergency Disaster Response and the Impact of the Media, the Military, and Time," *Defense & Foreign Affairs' Strategic Policy*, June 2005.

George Will "Leviathan in Louisiana," *Newsweek*, September 12, 2005.

Graham Wood "Tsunami Media Convergence: Not a Fair Guiding Principle for Aid," *Christian Science Monitor*, January 24, 2005.

Index

aid, 77, 80
  financial, is needed over food
    and goods, 95, 97–98, 99
  must be appropriate to local
    conditions, 96–97
  politicization of, 77–78
  transportation problems with,
    101–102
aid agencies. *See* nongovernmental
  organizations
aid fatigue, 80
Alaska Tsunami Warning Center,
  30
Alverson, Keith, 36

Bam (Iraq), 2003 earthquake in,
  80
barrier islands, 91
BBC News online, 119–20
Beaches Are Moving, The
  (Kaufman and Pilkey), 91
Bible, prophetic warnings in, 117–
  19, 120–21
Blair, Tony, 76, 77
Briceno, Salvano, 24
Brown, Gordon, 78
building codes, 8, 75, 90
Bush, David M., 82

Chakrabhand, Somchai, 63
Chertoff, Michael, 113
Clark, Ross, 48
coastal areas
  development in
    is based on market forces,
      85–86
    responsibilities of architects
      in, 87–88
  factors in management of,
    86–87
  population growth in, 83, 84

Coastal Barrier Resources Act,
  84–85
Coastal Zone Management Act, 84
Coquillon, Erzulie, 62
Courier-Post (newspaper), 70

Daily Express (newspaper), 120
Darwin, Charles, 37
Davis, Ian, 27
DDT, 107
Degg, Marin R., 8
DeGregori, Thomas R., 99
Department of Homeland Security
  (DHS), 110
developed nations, 80
developing nations, 46,78
development
  in coastal areas
    is based on market forces,
      85–86
    responsibilities of architects
      in, 87–88
    should be ecologically
      sound, 90–91
  in floodplains, should be
    stopped, 91–92
  may reduce effects of natural
    disasters, 52
    con, 70, 115–16
disaster management, local in-
  volvement in, 26, 66
disease prevention, 21
  technology and, 106–108
donors, education is needed for,
  98
drought, 15–16

earthquake(s), 73, 80
Earth Summit (Johannesburg,
  2002), 51
Economist (magazine), 76

Egeland, Jan, 25, 28, 77
Eisner, Richard K., 8

Federal Emergency Management Agency (FEMA), 110
federal government, disaster costs assumed by, 74
floods, 91, 120
    Hannibal, Missouri (1993), 66, 68–70
    Mozambique (2000), 81
Foiles, Virginia, 69
Foxcroft, Thomas, 72

Global Ocean Observing System (GOOS), 39
Global Sea Level Observing System (GLOSS), 39–40
global warming, 15, 120
    has preoccupied developed nations, 50, 51
God
    natural disasters as judgments of, 72–73
    Noah and, 117, 118

Hall, Donald, 72
Hannibal, Missouri 66, 68–70
Hewitt, Kenneth, 70
Houston Chronicle (newspaper), 100
humanitarian assistance, 77
    in natural disasters vs. complex emergencies, 15–17
    see also aid
Hurricane Hugo (1989), 75
Hurricane Katrina (2005), 9–10, 111
Hurricane Mitch (1998), 26, 80
hurricanes, 75, 82, 89
    see also specific hurricanes

Independent (newspaper), 115
India, 46
Indian Ocean, 34–35
Intergovernmental Oceanographic Commission (IOC), 37
international organizations. *See* nongovernmental organizations
International Recovery Platform (IRP), 27
International Strategy for Disaster Reduction (ISDR), 119
International Tsunami Information Center, 29, 30

Jarraud, Michel, 25
Jesus Christ, 118, 119
John (apostle), 119

Kaufman, Wallace, 91

Lean, Geoffrey, 115
Light, Paul, 109
Lomborg, Bjorn, 48, 50
Lyons, Charles J., 20

Maskrey, Andrew, 27
medicine, issues in delivery of, 102–103
Missouri, 73
mosquito-borne diseases, 107
Mount Nyirangongo eruption (2002), 11
    international response to, 12–13
    lessons learned from, 13–14
Mozambique, 81

Nagin, Ray, 112
National Flood Insurance Program, 85
National Tsunami Hazard Mitigation Program, 31

natural disasters, 44, 71, 81, 97
    aspects of response to, 111–12
    complex emergencies and,
        15–17
    deaths from, 15, 24, 26
    human development may re-
        duce effects of, 52
    con, 70, 115–16
Neal, William J., 82
needs assessment teams, 101
New Madrid fault earthquake
    (1811, 1812), 73
New York Times (newspaper), 64
Noah, 117–18
nongovernmental organizations
    (NGOs), 60, 65, 107
    are often best first responders,
        103–104
Nuland, Sherwin B., 53

ocean monitoring
    challenges of global system
        for, 40–41
    as part of tsunami warning
        system, 38–40
Office of Coordination of Hu-
    manitarian Affairs (OCHA), 13
oral rehydration therapy (ORT),
    105

Pacific Tsunami Warning System,
    30–31
Pagett, Donna, 69
Pan American Health Organiza-
    tion (PAHO), 95
Penick, James Lal, 73
Pentecost Island, 1999 tsunami on,
    32–33
Peppiatt, David, 9, 10
Persson, Goran, 49
Peter (apostle), 118
Pilkey, Orrin, 91
post-traumatic stress disorder, 57,
    62

poverty, 55
    link between disasters and, 26,
        44–45, 49
Powell, Colin, 77–78
prevention, disaster, 28, 46, 81
ProVention Consortium, 9

Reice, Seth R., 89
Roy, Suprakash, 43

Schroeder, John Ross, 114
sea levels, 39, 40
Sparks, Peter, 75
Sri Lanka, 59
    Tamil rebellion in, 60–61, 64
    tsunami victims in, 54–55
Steinberg, Ted, 66
storm surges, 38
Sumathipala, Athula, 64
Sunday Telegraph (newspaper),
    115
Sunday Times (newspaper), 115
Synolakis, Costas, 29

Tearfund, 81
Time (magazine), 75
Todd, Shellia, 69
Tsui, Ed, 11
tsunami(s), 8, 29, 47
    2004 South Asian, 7, 20–22,
        63, 78
    lack of warning of, 32–33,
        116–17

UNESCO, 30, 33, 37, 42
UN Global Early Warning Pro-
    gramme, 25
UNICEF (United Nations Chil-
    dren's Fund), 19
UN Millennium Declaration, 80
USA Today (newspaper), 115
U.S. Geological Survey, 81

Van de Wetering, Maxine, 73

victims, disaster, 95
    counseling for, 58, 63–64
    psycho-physiological symptoms exhibited by, 53, 56

Vietnam, mitigation against typhoons in, 8–9

Ville de Goyet, Claude de, 94

Voyage of the Beagle (Darwin), 37

warning systems, tsunami, 7–8, 25, 29
    better communications are needed in, 45–46
    history of, 30–31
    innovations of, 31–32
    need for, in Indian Ocean, 34–35

    should include storm surge surveillance, 38–39

Weinstein, Stuart, 115, 116

Williamson, Bob, 68

Wisner, Ben, 24, 25

World Bank, 27, 45

World Conference on Disaster Reduction (2005), 23
    initiatives announced at, 27–28

Wright, Sharon, 120

Young, Emma, 23

Young, Robert S., 82

zoning, ecologically based, 90